Pick is dedicated to each individual who longs for more and courageously pursues a life of peace, purpose and passion. May you be richly rewarded and use your experiences to help others.

Acknowledgements

A special thanks to Mom, Dad and Charlene. You've encouraged me, gently told me the truth and proofed and reproofed my work. I am profoundly grateful. Thank you for living your values every day and for your love, prayers and encouragement. To Russ, Bob, Madison and Ryan. Your encouragement, excitement and prayers were invaluable. To Danie, thank you for showing me how much a dedicated and determined doer can accomplish.

To Elizabeth Rawls, thanks for the meaningful conversations and brainstorming over the decades, for your enduring friendship and for working through every speed bump our relationship has ever encountered. Light bulbs go off every time we chat and as we both chase our dreams.

To Barb Dunn, thanks for your treasured friendship and for sharing your heart, God-given talents and life with me. Your prayers and encouragement are invaluable. To Nancy Barnes, your friendship is ever so dear and you've taught me much through the years.

To the book party crews, I enjoyed seeing each of you curled up reading. It's a much better book because of your honesty, encouragement and insights—Anita Gross, Ann Owens, Barb Dunn, Betty Schumacher, Crina Tarasi, Daun Neff, Debbie Lukens, Diane Lucka, Kayla Slezak, Kelley

Elzroth, Jan King, Jana Rowland, Jennifer Wirz, Joyce Reynhout, Leatha Olsen, Lori Driessnack, Mary Cross, Nancy Barnes, Suann Sheahan and Robyn Wickes.

To Andy Cheely, Bill Linder, Brian Lamew, Jason Raitz, Jill Howard, Lawrence Gross, Jason Bentley and Jon Robb. Thanks for the encouragement and wisdom each of you shared.

To my counseling students at Central Michigan University. Thanks for encouraging me, holding me gently accountable and believing in my dreams. Having you cheer me on made the journey far less lonely.

To my friends, the staff and the Thursday morning prayer group at Mt. Pleasant Community Church, as well as Gina Umpstead, Frannie Medders and Tracy Oneale who prayed for me week after week. Thank you.

To Joni McPherson for creating a cover I love. To Dianne Morr for your encouragement, editing and getting the manuscript ready for publication. I couldn't have done it without you.

To Dr. Brenda Freeman for showing me grace, mentoring me and teaching me so much. I wouldn't be where I am today without you. To Dr. Ken Coll for changing my life through what you taught and the tough conversations we shared.

To Mark LeBlanc for teaching me high value activities and helping me move beyond dreaming into doing. To Sam Horn for teaching me to share my stories and helping make the chapters flow. To Dr. Debra Smilo, Dr. Brian Sanborn and Barb Sloan for helping me overcome the things that threatened to delay and derail my success.

Table of Contents

Introduction

Passionate about helping others develop healthier relationships and a happier life, I learned long ago that while you don't always get to pick what happens to you, you do get to pick your response. You can either be miserable or marvelous. Obviously, marvelous is better.

Pick is written to empower you to create a life you love and to overcome what holds you back. *Pick* contains the insights I've discovered through life's trials and triumphs, as well as the lessons and techniques I've learned as a licensed professional counselor and counselor educator.

Each chapter starts with a story from my life: some funny, some raw, some embarrassing. Used to illustrate key points, the stories are intended to help you to see yourself more clearly and to encourage you to push past what prevents you from living your best life.

Pick

I've battled bulimia, been depressed and feared my own shadow. I've been humiliated, bullied and dumped without explanation. I've clung to security, stunted my growth and gotten stuck. I've lost someone I loved to suicide. My roommate was raped and murdered.

Yet I have chosen forgiveness over bitterness, faith over fear and growth over giving up. You can too.

While I have encountered great pain, I am not a victim. I am stronger, wiser and kinder.

I am peaceful.

I am purposeful.

I am powerful.

You can be too.

Some days I sprint towards my dreams, other days I limp. Some days I sit on the sidelines. It is then that I must determine what I value, want and am willing to fight for. I've come to know myself well, my strengths and stumbling blocks, my passions and my purpose.

I will not slip silently into the night. I will not live a second rate life. I will not give up. While I can't control the outcomes, I get to choose my attitudes and actions.

I pick to live a life of integrity.

I pick to live life to the fullest.

I pick to be happy.

You can too.

It isn't always easy.

What about you? Are you living a life you love? Are you pursuing your passions and purpose? Do you dare to dream and achieve the audacious? Are you moving forward, emanating excitement and drawing opportunities like moths to a flame?

Or, are you selling yourself short? Are you living with the dull ache of dashed dreams? Are you trapped by fear, frustration or faulty thinking? Is pain pinning you down? Do you lack the mindset and behaviors you need to create the life you desire?

Worse yet, have you accepted defeat? Have you settled for less than what you know you deserve? Does your heart still long for more?

I've long wondered why some prevail while others fail. Mired in the muck and bogged down by disappointment, despair or depression, many blame circumstances and bad luck. Years slip away. Dreams get deferred.

While it is true that some have a much harder life than others, no one goes through their journey unscathed. Life isn't fair, bad things happen and time takes its toll. Despite their impact, circumstances don't define or control you unless you allow them to.

The good news is, no matter what's happened in your past, your upbringing, your employment, your marital status, your weight or the size of your bank account, you can transform your life.

Pick is your invitation to overcome what's holding you back. Anchored on awareness, acceptance, action and accountability, *Pick* will help you develop the mindset and skills you need to build the life you desire.

Complain or create?

Frustrated or fulfilled?

Pick

Dreamer or doer?

Passive or powerful?

Miserable or marvelous?

Pick.

Pick is my heart for you. Rather than reading it and stashing it away, I hope it finds a home on your desk or nightstand. If you have an audio copy, play it when you're driving, doing chores or getting ready for your day.

Use it to pick proactive attitudes and behaviors. Use it to overcome turmoil. Use it to pick up the pace on realizing your potential.

Pick to make today and everyday more of what you want and less of what you don't.

Pick to fulfill your dreams.

Pick to create a life you love.

Sherene McHenry, Ph.D., LPC

Sherene@ShereneMcHenry.com

Chapter 1

Stuck or Soaring: Get Moving

"Keep your focus on things you can actually control. Choosing to center on anything else will either stop you in your tracks or significantly slow you down."
Sherene McHenry

Sometimes I get stuck.

I recently returned from a lovely vacation. Seven sundrenched days filled with loved ones, laughter and lightheartedness. We played games. We rode the waves. We walked the beach. I returned energized and ready to take on the world.

Then, I crashed. For four days I did nothing. I didn't write. I didn't unpack. I didn't work on my book. I didn't even do the dishes. Instead, I became a zombie zoning out in front of the television. Bet you're wondering if you want to keep reading. Please do.

Pick

What went wrong? How did I go from happy and energized to bogged down and burdened?

For starters, I spent most of the summer sick. From catching MRSA in Hawaii and an infection in Hong Kong to contracting a bug at the beach on the mainland, I took seven consecutive rounds of prescription medicine. My body wasn't happy. Neither was I.

It's easy to get discouraged and distracted when I'm not feeling well or operating at full capacity.

But my health struggles are only part of the story. Emotional quicksand also dragged me down and threatened to engulf me this summer.

A loved one committed suicide in the spring. Her beauty, creativity and potential instantly and forever silenced. Our hopes and hearts splintered into tiny shards.

If that weren't enough, a close relationship derailed leaving me feeling battered, bruised and betrayed. Instead of being invested in creativity, my energy turned inward as I tried to make sense of what went wrong.

Like a broken record, my thoughts looped and re-looped as I internally rehashed events and rehearsed conversations. Regardless of how much I processed, the rift remained. I was stuck.

What was changing, however, was my life.

Drastically.

After almost two decades, I was transitioning from being a professor with a steady paycheck to being a full-time speaker, writer, consultant and success coach. Leaving a good job that I did well was simultaneously terrifying and exciting. Desire that once whispered screamed like a siren.

I was excited.

It was time.

It was what I was created to do.

It was what I dreamed of for over a decade.

It was what I labored and sacrificed for.

It was a big leap of faith.

It was frightening.

Fear tried to wrap its fingers around my future.

"Give up on your dreams," it invited. "Play it safe. You have a great job. Times are tough. It's stupid to risk. Not everyone's cut out to be a business owner."

I've long been susceptible to fear.

As a child, it terrified me to have to go downstairs and turn off the lights. *The Wizard of Oz* gave me nightmares. I worried the people I loved would die.

Fear followed me forward. As I got older I worried about being liked and looking stupid. I worried about what I should or shouldn't do. I worried about my safety. I worried whether I'd succeed. Apprehension, like a dark cloud, hovered nearby.

Despite my fears, I lived, loved and laughed. Staying busy helped keep my fears at bay.

In my mid-twenties my anxieties and maladaptive coping strategies caught up with me. Saddened and stuck, I entered therapy. It was there I learned to face my fears and to pick to focus on the things I could actually impact. Fear took a back seat. The dark cloud diminished.

Pick

Wanting to help others, I headed cross country to pursue my doctorate in counseling the following year. Two weeks in, I got the call.

"Melinda's dead."

My roommate had been raped and murdered. Beautiful, funny, full of promise, Melinda was gone.

Fear crashed back in, engulfing me fully.

Going back for her funeral was excruciating. I was terrified her parents would blame me. Thankfully, my fears were unfounded. Despite unbearable pain, they affirmed our friendship and the fun we'd shared.

I returned to school in horrible shape.

Frightened of my own shadow, I'd stay up until the wee hours of the morning hoping to fall asleep the moment my head hit the pillow. Exhaustion became a constant companion.

Feeling like a jagged piece of glass that would either shatter or slice should anyone get too close, I isolated myself. A hazy fog engulfed me.

Knowing I needed help, I tried counseling two times. Neither therapist was helpful. What I desperately needed was a trauma specialist. I didn't know they existed.

So I limped along, doing the best I could. No one, including myself, understood the changes in me. People wanted me to be my old self. So did I.

I couldn't do it.

After about eight months, the fog began to lift. I made new friends, changed jobs and focused on finishing my degree. Beside the fact that I'd put on a lot of weight and lived life in a heightened state of alert, I appeared normal. Especially to those who hadn't known me before the tragedy.

I graduated and experienced success in many areas of my life becoming a full professor, writing a textbook, speaking around the world, and enjoying fulfilling relationships. I even bought a lovely old farm house.

My fears, however, refused to subside.

So, I found ways to cope. I put electronic candles in the windows to chase away the daily darkness. I installed an alarm system. I prayed.

Nightly, I asked God to be the God of my dreams and requested angels for protection. Turning out the light, I'd wink at the rocker beside my bed and thank my indoor angel. It made me smile. More importantly, I slept soundly, something I hadn't done in over a decade.

Fourteen years after Melinda's death, I found a trauma therapist. In six short sessions she restored my shattered sense of safety. While I still get frightened and anxious on occasion, I no longer live in fear. I am free.

Through it all I've learned that being stuck is an indicator something is wrong. Instead of viewing being stuck as the problem, I've learned it's simply a warning signal like the check engine light on a dashboard. The sooner I figure out what the problem is, the quicker I can take action. I'm most likely to get stuck when:

♦ I focus too far into the future.
♦ I focus on things I can't control.
♦ I have a rift in a relationship.
♦ I don't know what to do.

Pick

- ♦ I get run down.
- ♦ I get overwhelmed.
- ♦ I feel fearful.

Like sand enables a stuck tire to take traction, telling myself the truth about where I am and figuring out what's holding me back positions me to move forward.

I've also learned that change requires action. While knowing what's wrong is a great start, if I want unstuck, I must move beyond insight into action.

Sometimes all I have to do is pray and I'm able to move. Fast, simple, powerful. I love it when it's that easy.

Other times I need to take a specific action. For example, when something's wrong in a relationship, I can initiate a conversation, choose to forgive or set appropriate boundaries. If I'm run down, I can take better care of myself. If I'm overwhelmed, I can focus on the next step instead of the whole project.

It's when I fail to take action that I shrink my life and waste precious time and energy going around in circles. In doing so, I risk delaying or destroying my dreams.

> *Getting stuck is reactive,*
> *taking action is proactive.*

The quicker I seek assistance when I can't get unstuck, the happier and more productive I am. There are times when no matter how hard I try I can't figure things out on my own. I've found when I share my concerns with someone I trust, I can almost always get moving again.

6

Just today I called a dear friend and said, "I'm stuck on where to go with the book. Will you let me talk about it, see if I can come up with where I need to go, and tell me if you have any insights?"

Elizabeth listened patiently and compassionately then offered some brilliant insights. Unstuck, I promptly went back to work.

There are also times I need professional help. Experts continue to enrich my life, cut down my learning curve and help me accomplish my hopes and dreams. For example, I work with a consultant who helps me grow my business. I attend conferences. I read self-help books.

In the aftermath of the suicide, I felt myself spiraling towards a dark place. Recognizing it as similar to my reaction after Melinda's murder, I immediately started working with a trauma therapist.

She taught me to replace the horrific, morbid thoughts running through my head with a single, specific memory of the person I loved. It works. While I still have sorrow, those horrifying thoughts no longer overtake me. When such thoughts resurface, I quickly replace them and regain my sense of balance.

What about you? Are you stuck? Are you fearful? Is your past holding you back? Are present circumstances weighing you down? Have you stalled on reaching your dreams? Are you ready to get moving again?

If you want to get unstuck there are three things you can do immediately:

Pick

1. **Tell yourself the truth about being stuck.** It's not shameful to get stuck nor does getting stuck mean you're a bad person or failure. Getting stuck simply means you've got a problem that needs to be addressed if you want to keep moving and create a life you love.

You begin to break the chains holding you back the moment you tell yourself the truth about what's going on.

> *Getting stuck isn't the problem.*
> *Staying stuck is.*

You are brave and strong enough to face the truth. Freedom and your future await you.

2. **Once you've told yourself the truth, tell someone else.** Sometimes all it takes is talking to a trusted friend to get moving again. If you don't have one, or talking with one isn't enough to jumpstart you to action, call in the pros. You can eliminate years of struggling by working with a counselor, life coach, consultant or pastor.

If you're suffering from trauma, work with a trauma specialist. Had I found one after Melinda's murder, I wouldn't have needlessly lived 14 years in fear. I also would have been happier and had more energy to devote to living life to the fullest and fulfilling my dreams.

Once you get up the courage to talk to someone, you'll be tempted to edit out the ugly parts. Don't do it. Keeping secrets keeps you stuck.

It's beyond embarrassing to admit I've zoned out and watched television for days on end. Admitting it helps prevent me from picking to do it again and again.

Silence traps and isolates.
Sharing lightens the load and heals.

Your life is waiting. Don't keep it on hold with fear or pride.

3. **Focus on things you can control.** Fear immobilizes, and all the worry in the world can't change circumstances, outcomes or events. Fear and worry will never get you where you want to go. They'll only rob you of your joy, your energy and ultimately your health.

Instead of living in fear and worrying about things over which you have no control, concentrate your energy and efforts on the things you actually have the power to impact. Master this and you're well on your way to soaring.

The Serenity Prayer

God grant me the serenity to accept the things I cannot change, courage to change the things I can and wisdom to know the difference.

Reinhold Neibuhr

The following chart provides examples to help you zero in on the facets of life over which you have control. At the end of the day, the only thing you have the power to fully control is yourself and what you pick to do.

Control Comparison Chart

Things You Can't Control	Things You Can Control
A terrorist attack	Being a concerned citizen
Who is elected	If you vote
World events	The charities you support and the products you buy
The news	How much news you watch
"Weather Gone Wild"	If your insurance is up to date
The economy	Your savings and debt load
Paying taxes	If you maximize your deductions
How others spend their resources	How you spend your resources
Who others choose as friends	Who you choose as friends
How others spend their day	How you spend your day
If everyone likes you	How you treat others
If you'll win	If you do your best
If you'll be promoted	How hard you work
If others pursue their dreams	If you pursue yours

Worry and fear are not your friends. If you want to create a life you love, you can't afford to stay stuck or to focus on things you can't control.

Pick to get moving.

Pick to control your thoughts and actions.

Pick to create the life you deserve and desire.

Chapter 2
Lies or Truth:
Get Real

*"Let us dare to be ourselves, for we do that
better than anyone else can."*

Shirley Briggs

I was living a lie.

It started innocently enough. I was standing in front
of the mirror stretching my neck hoping to tone my chin.

I'd recently learned my college was implementing
weight limits for cheerleaders. As I studied myself, mouth
opening and shutting like a baby bird waiting for her mother,
I decided I'd lose weight by throwing up.

Thus began my dark descent. Oh, it didn't start out
badly. For the first three months I felt in control, my weight
dropped and I got more "You look great" compliments and
dates than I'd ever had.

Pick

When questioned, "How did you lose the weight?" I'd reply, "I just stopped eating." Nothing could have been further from the truth. I'd eat a normal meal then head straight to the bathroom.

About three months in, I distinctly remember thinking, "It doesn't matter what I eat, I'm going to throw it all up anyway." That day I began to binge in earnest. Bags of cookies, a gallon of ice cream, multiple desserts, chips…

If I was stressed, I binged. If I was happy, I binged. If I was sad or mad, I binged.

I lived my life draped over one dirty toilet bowl after another. My clothing, routinely soiled from toilet splatter, spoke of my secret.

Laxatives became a part of life. So did weighing myself multiple times a day. Ever fluctuating yet never good enough, I tied my self-esteem to a bathroom scale.

The most humiliating part of each week was weigh-in. In dread, I'd wear my lightest clothing, take off my shoes and jewelry and manipulate the number by a quarter of a pound by leaning just so.

To the casual observer my world looked good. I cheered for four years, was student government president, got to hang out with former United States President, Jimmy Carter, was homecoming honor attendant and regularly made the Dean's List.

But no one knew the real me. Not even me. Cheerful by nature and forever on the go, I rarely slowed down long enough for any of my feelings to surface. About the only time they bubbled up was when I was in the Dean of Women's office.

To my confusion, I'd start crying for no apparent reason. My standard response was to say, "I don't know why I'm crying, I'm happy," dry my tears and head over to the cafeteria. And yes, you guessed it, binge and purge away any remaining feelings.

Once, my roommate had a small bag of M&M's on her desk. I ate them, planning to replace them. Unfortunately, they were a gift from her boyfriend that she'd proudly displayed. It's one of the few times I ever saw her truly ticked off. I imagine she hid food after that.

Cheerleading ended and I graduated. Unfortunately, my bulimia followed me through my master's program and into my first job.

Just as in college, my life looked good. I was cheerful, had a great job and owned my home. I kept my doubt, isolation and pain at bay with busyness and bulimia.

Over time, the bulimia began to backfire. I'd gorge myself, but started putting off throwing up. Naturally, I gained weight. Loathing myself, I'd look in the mirror, eyes full of hatred and disgust. "You ate it. You deserve to be fat."

Life began to slowly crumble around me. I became increasingly depressed, dreaded my job and had few friends.

Eventually I sought help at an eating disorder clinic. Not because I thought there was anything wrong with throwing up or my life, but because I was desperate to lose weight.

Pick

I cried the entire intake session. Just as in college, I kept saying, "I don't know why I'm crying. I'm happy."

All evidence pointed to the contrary. I just didn't know how to tell myself the truth, let alone be honest with anyone else.

About two weeks in, my group therapist, none too gently I might add, invited me to get real. "You're great at giving advice, Sherene, but you share nothing of yourself."

Infuriated, embarrassed and put on the spot, I wanted to rush home, binge and purge it back up. I had no idea how I felt about things, and I certainly wasn't comfortable sharing my life and struggles with strangers.

While not overly eager to do so, I did open up. As I began to tell myself and my group members the truth about my life, I discovered I was hurt, angry and isolated.

I'll never forget the first time I heard Wayne Watson's song, *Friend of a Wounded Heart:*

"Smile, make them think you're happy.
Laugh and say that things are fine.
And hide that empty longing that you feel.
Don't ever show it; just keep your heart concealed..."

The music and his words hauntingly described my life. Only I hadn't just hidden my heart from others, I'd hidden it from myself.

I get hurt.

I get angry.

I get frustrated.

I used to think feeling negative emotions meant I was bad, broken or needy. They don't. They simply signify I'm human. Instead of hiding my feelings under lock and key from myself and others, I learned to slow down and allow myself to feel them fully.

Pain reminds me that I care and have a tender heart. It also makes me sensitive to how I treat others.

While not pleasant, anger is an appropriate response to injustice. Anger is also inevitable. What matters is how anger is handled. Specifically, it is never ok to hurt yourself or others, no matter how angry or justified you feel.

Therapy also taught me to gently tell others the truth about how their behavior, intentional or not, impacts me. For example, "It hurts me when I'm left out," "It frustrates me when I'm repeatedly interrupted," and "It saddens me when I'm not given a chance to change or explain."

I also learned to tell myself the truth about what I wanted and what I did and didn't like. For example, although I had a great job, it wasn't a good fit for me. I wasn't happy doing it, I was continually working out of my weaknesses instead of my strengths, and I didn't feel fulfilled. My love was teaching others. It still is.

Was my journey to authenticity easy? No. Did it happen overnight? No. I did months of therapy, cried buckets of tears and allowed myself to get angry.

It was scary.

It was liberating.

I became real.

Pick

I know who I am, what I like and what makes me happy, sad, anxious and angry. I speak truth as gently as I can and allow others the freedom to tell me how I impact them as well.

It's been almost a quarter of a century since I entered therapy. Far from stress free, my life has had ups and downs and times of excruciating pain. Being real with myself, others and even God has kept me from returning to binging and purging's vicious cycle. I am forever grateful for the lessons I learned.

What about you? Do you know yourself well? Do you allow yourself to feel? Do you let others know the real you? Or do you hide, chameleon like, ever morphing into what someone else desires?

Do you struggle to tell yourself and others the truth about your likes and dislikes, pet peeves, hopes and dreams, what you value and what you are and are not willing to do? Do you long to be more peaceful, powerful and purposeful?

Take heart. With one ounce of courage, it is possible to become real. Here are four key steps:

1. Embrace the fact that you don't have to be perfect for people to like you. Instead of ensuring others will like you, the pretense of perfection repels people. First, as no one is perfect, they know the facade can't be real, and secondly it's intimidating. Who wants to be around a perfect person who never messes up?

Our imperfections draw others to us not plastic illusions of flawlessness.

Once you give up trying to be or appear perfect, you'll find others like you far better. People are drawn to individuals who laugh at themselves and invite the world to laugh with them.

When I first became a professor, I was knowledgeable and helpful, but not very well liked by my students. It wasn't until I began to tell the embarrassing stories of my journey that students began to identify with and appreciate me.

One of my most mortifying experiences happened the first time a couple I was counseling told me they were having sex problems. Much to my horror, I got the nervous giggles.

It wasn't one giggle and get back to business. No, I turned red, put my head down and giggled for what seemed like an eternity. All I could repeatedly choke out was, "I'm sorry. I promise I'm not laughing at you."

I'll never forget the look of horror and confusion on their faces.

Like a deer caught in headlights, I was completely unprepared. I'd grown up in a family where, beyond the birds and bees talk, sex simply wasn't mentioned. And, I must have missed the day they taught that couples would want help with sex problems. It was a nightmare.

Why do I tell my students that story? First, to illustrate that they don't have to be perfect to become good counselors and that they too will make mistakes along the way. It also illustrates that clients are resilient, especially when counselors are authentic and apologize when they mess up.

Pick

That couple stayed with me, allowing me access to the most private parts of their life and the joy of helping them create a rewarding relationship.

2. **Turn hide into seek.** If you want to create a life you love, instead of hiding from who you are and how you feel, seek to know yourself well. Make it your quest to uncover your likes and dislikes, strengths and weaknesses, the person you are today and the person you desire to become.

If you don't already know, figure out what makes you tick and what makes you happy, angry and sad. Instead of wondering if you *"should"* be feeling something, allow yourself to feel your feelings. Feelings aren't good or bad, they're just feelings. Your response is what matters.

3. **Gently tell yourself and others the truth.** Until you know yourself well, this is extremely difficult to do. In addition to knowing yourself and being able to acknowledge how you feel, gentle truth telling takes true courage and commitment. Tell the truth:

♦ If you don't want to do something.
♦ If you don't like something.
♦ If you don't need or want something.
♦ If you're stuck.
♦ If you're afraid.
♦ If you're happy, sad or angry.

For example, a friend recently bailed out on a long planned ski outing hours before we were supposed to leave. Having looked forward to the trip immensely, I was hurt, angry, and disappointed.

Instead of silently seething or pretending everything was fine, I shared that my feelings were hurt and that I was disappointed and frustrated. She apologized and committed to holding future plans more carefully. Now, instead of still being angry, I'm looking forward to the next time we're able to ski.

4. Send clear messages. When you tell the truth, it's critical that you send clear messages. If you're like most, you've been socialized from an early age to hide your thoughts and emotions by sending mixed messages.

Mixed messages include laughing when things aren't funny, walking on egg shells, saying things tentatively, and beating around the bush in the hope your message gets through. The problem with mixed messages is that they doom you to being discounted, misunderstood and frustrated.

While teaching a human relations course in Atlanta, I had a beautiful, twenty something, classic southern belle as one of my students. Every day, an equally attractive young man sat beside her.

When I'd approach her side of the class, be it during a break or a small group assignment, in her smooth southern drawl she'd giggle, "Dr. Sherene, he's bothering me. Make him stop."

Trained in sexual harassment, I double and triple checked to see if she meant it. "Yes, he's bothering me," was her standard reply, "Make him stop, tee hee hee."

While I found the exchanges disconcerting, I repeatedly concluded that they were flirting and she liked

Pick

him. Expecting to soon hear they'd started dating, I'd go back to teaching, confident she wasn't being harassed.

Near the end of the second weekend, I taught about the importance of sending clear messages. The gist of the lecture? That if they wanted to be heard and taken seriously their voice tone needed to match their face, words and body language.

At break I approached her side of the room. With a serious voice tone and no smile, she looked me square in the eye and said, "He is bothering me. Make him stop."

You could have knocked me over with a feather. She'd been asking for help, but her mixed messages had caused me to discount her distress.

I promptly intervened, not that I needed to at that point. The shock on his face left no doubt that he too had finally understood that she did not welcome his advances and was to leave her alone.

What caused the communication failure? The simple fact that words alone don't constitute communication. The truth is, far more is conveyed through your voice tone and body language than through the words you say.

According to communications expert, Dr. Albert Mehrabian, when it comes to interpreting the feelings and attitudes of others, we rely on three key pieces of information to decode interactions and determine what's really being said:

♦ **Nonverbal Information**

Approximately 55% of what people believe to be truth is determined by nonverbals. If you tell someone you're upset, but you're smiling because you're nervous or want to soften the verbal blow, they aren't going to believe you. End of story.

♦ **Voice Tone**

Roughly 38% of what's relied on for incoming information is voice tone. If you're giggling and sound cheerful while saying you're upset, you will be discounted. Again, end of story.

♦ **Words**

What you say only accounts for about 7% of what's believed in any message conveying feelings or attitude. Saying "He's bothering me, make him stop," with a giggle completely drowned out the words and left the impression that things were actually fine. Why? Because everything but the words screamed the opposite was true.

If your words don't match your nonverbals or voice tone, people aren't going to accurately hear or believe what you're saying. In order to be fully heard, your face, voice tone and words must match.

> *If you want to be trusted and taken seriously, your face, voice tone and words must match.*

Please note I don't have anything against laughing. It's the mixed message of laughing when you're upset that prevents others from truly hearing you.

I hope you'll laugh often, loud and long when you're happy and that you'll give others the gift of joining in their

Pick

joy. By the same token, I hope you'll allow yourself to weep when things are sad and join others in their pain.

I also hope you'll allow yourself to get angry when there's injustice. In fact, I hope your anger motivates you to do all that is within your power to make things right for yourself or for someone else in need. There may be a time you'll need someone to advocate for you.

What matters when you're angry is how you act. Raging, the silent treatment or cutting someone out of your life without giving them an opportunity to change only cause more pain and problems.

Laugh when things are funny.
Cry when things are sad.
Get angry at injustice.

While it's hard to tell yourself and others the truth, it frees everyone involved to make better decisions and to move forward with integrity and confidence.

Pick to feel.

Pick to tell the truth.

Pick to be powerful.

Chapter 3

Naysayers or Yeasayers: Form Fantastic Friendships

"The quality of a life is reflected in the quality of one's relationships."
Sherene McHenry

I ran into Dave one day, a fellow professor I'd known for years. We'd served together on several committees, completed a joint project and ran into each other on a regular basis.

"How's the book coming?" he asked.

"Painfully slow," I bemoaned.

Hoping for a bit of encouragement I elaborated. "It takes me anywhere from 40 to 60 hours to complete a single chapter."

Pick

"Maybe you shouldn't be a writer," he replied.

Shock froze my face. Dead silence ensued. A cold chill threatened to douse my dreams. I don't remember what I said. I do remember feeling confused, misjudged and unsupported.

Shortly thereafter another acquaintance asked the same question. "How's the book coming?"

"Slowly," I answered more cautiously this time.

"You know, Sherene, if it's taking this long, maybe you're not supposed to write the book."

Ouch.

Hearing it the first time had been hard. Getting torn down twice was terrible. I walked away feeling deflated, discouraged and disheartened. Doubt crashed in, flooding me with questions.

What's wrong with me? Am I a bad writer? Are my dreams too lofty? Do I complain too much? Was I foolish to tell people I was writing a book? Should I give up on writing and pack away my dreams?

Despite the cloud of confusion, I was unwilling to abandon my belief that I could help people around the world with a well-written book.

So I plodded along and began to learn about the world of publishing. I found out all I needed to approach the publisher of my dreams was three completed chapters and a book proposal.

I worked hard polishing my writing. My mother and my sister proofed my work. Knowing I'd done my best, I sent off my proposal with a prayer.

Anxiously awaiting a response, I anticipated the validation an acceptance letter would bring and the doors it would open. I was excited. I was expectant. I was apprehensive. After months of waiting, the response arrived.

"Thanks, but no thanks."

The rejection stung. I cried. I'd aimed for the stars and come up short. Maybe the naysayers were right. Maybe I shouldn't be writing a book.

That night I met my friends for dinner. "Can I tell you my sad tale of woe?" I blurted before I even sat down. Wide-eyed, they nodded their heads in assent.

With a tear rolling down my left cheek and quivering chin, I sadly shared, "My book got rejected. I got the letter today."

In unison, they jumped to their feet, hugged me and peppered me with the following comments:

"That's one editor's opinion."

"Don't give up, pal. John Grisham and J. K. Rowling were rejected multiple times."

"*Chicken Soup for the Soul* was rejected too."

"You're going to be famous."

"They'll be sorry they passed on your book."

Buoyed by their loyalty and immersed in their encouragement, I wiped away my tears, had a great evening, and kept on writing. You hold the finished product in your hands.

I learned a great deal through that experience. First, I need to be careful who I let close to my heart and my dreams. There are people who will tear me down, trample on my dreams and ask me to live a lesser life. They are entitled to their opinion.

Others build me up, affirm my dreams and spur me on when the going gets tough. They believe in me. They want the best for me. They are on my team. They are entitled to a part of my heart.

I am blessed to be a *pearl girl*, part of the group of women who rallied around me that night. The *pearls* are yeasayers, characterized by kindness, courage and character. Each pursues her dreams and is unfailingly supportive. While our lives and dreams differ significantly, our hearts are carbon copies.

I am a better person because of the *pearls* and other yeasayers in my life. They listen, enlighten and encourage. They pick me up. They celebrate my success. What a gift.

> *Yeasayers are*
> *priceless pearls.*

Feedback is not all equal, nor is it always valid. My yeasayers helped me press forward and write a better book. The naysayers nudged me towards a smaller life.

The fact of the matter is the typical nonfiction book takes approximately 750 hours to write. My 40 to 60 hours a chapter were in the ballpark, not an indicator my dreams were too lofty or that I shouldn't be a writer.

> *Don't blindly accept another's opinion.*
> *Find the facts.*

Naysayers or Yeasayers

People give feedback based on who they are and what they believe. Yeasayers tend to take risks and follow their own dreams. As a result, they encourage others to do the same.

Many naysayers have good hearts and view themselves as realists who don't want anyone to get hurt. Others are less healthy and delight in knocking dreamers down. Either way, it is often difficult for naysayers to be supportive.

It's wise to strategically determine the access I allow others into the sensitive parts of my soul. Like gardeners of fragile flowers, yeasayers nurture and protect. In contrast, naysayers trample, damage and destroy.

Hearts, hopes and dreams can be incredibly delicate, especially in their infancy. Be careful who you allow to access them.

What about you? What type of people do you let close to your heart? Are you surrounded by people who douse your dreams and cause you doubt? Do you find yourself on the receiving end of dismissive and caustic comments? Are others ridiculing or diminishing your hopes and dreams?

Or, do you have individuals you can count on to cheer you on? Are there people in your life who rally around you, believe in you and pick you up when you're down? Do you have people who let you grow and who encourage you to be your best self?

Pick

If you long to be surrounded by supportive yeasayers, the following ideas will help you identify who to let into the inner circles of your life:

1. **Parade and confetti throwers.** I strongly encourage you to seek out individuals who will celebrate your success. Look for people generous with their enthusiasm, excitement and encouragement.

My sister is a fantastic parade and confetti thrower. She's emotionally generous and never fails to get excited when good things happen in my life. Her joy, enthusiasm, and belief in me boost my confidence and help me press forward when the going gets tough.

The opposite occurs when someone throws a wet blanket on your happiness. My first experience with this was at the tender age of eight when I won my first, first place in a gymnastics meet. I was so excited.

A teammate quickly crushed the glow of my accomplishment. "You only won because you didn't do anything hard and didn't fall off," she snarled. I wasn't wise enough at the time to consider the source. As a result, I lost some of my confidence and joy.

The same girl continued to make hurtful remarks for the next ten years. I wish I had known then what I know now. If someone isn't ready, willing or able to celebrate your joy it tells you something about them, not about you.

2. **People who make you laugh and bring you joy.** You have a choice with whom you spend your time. I highly suggest surrounding yourself with individuals who make you laugh and bring you joy.

Find people who readily laugh at life and at themselves as well. Up your game and do the same. As your life resounds with laughter and joy, you'll have far more energy to devote to creating a life you love.

3. People who join in your joy and sorrow and allow you the freedom to be angry. Equally important to cultivating relationships with individuals who make you laugh is finding friends who allow you to feel all of your emotions.

Even better are friends capable of joining you where you are. Shared happiness multiplies joy. Shared sorrow lessens pain. Acknowledged anger decreases the pain and injustice of maltreatment.

Just today I was feeling marginalized and blindsided after a meeting. As we walked, I filled my neighbor in on what had occurred.

"Unbelievable," was her empathic response.

She didn't try to talk me out of my feelings, begin to analyze me or make excuses for what had happened. She simply let me be angry. As a result my frustration lowered.

It's important to note that while healthy individuals allow others to feel their full range of emotions, they don't tolerate or accept abuse.

4. People you admire and respect. You position yourself to live your best life when you surround yourself with individuals you respect and admire. Those actively pursuing their dreams will encourage you to do so as well. Those who are wise will encourage you to make good choices. Those who prize strong relationships will help you protect and invest in your key relationships.

Pick

On the flip side, those who wait for life to happen will encourage you to rest on your laurels. Those lacking in wisdom will encourage you to act rashly. Those without good character will teach you to cut corners.

> *Choose wisely who you allow to influence you.*

5. People who genuinely like you and light up in your presence. Seek out relationships with individuals who perk up when you're around and who like you for being you. They provide a natural energy boost and buffer from the world.

My friend Elizabeth and I clicked the first time we met, and almost 20 years later we've yet to run out of things to talk about. She's fiercely loyal, laughs at my jokes and loves me simply for being me. Who wouldn't want to be around someone like that?

On the flip side are people who are ambivalent towards you, don't like you or are never going to like you.

New to a job, I had a coworker ask me to go for a walk. Knowing she was reaching out and that her own transition had been difficult, I accepted her gracious invitation.

As we drove to the park, I became increasingly uncomfortable. She was quite an introvert and I didn't want to get on her nerves. The silence became deafening. It took everything I had not to start giggling. I would never have been able to stop.

We finally arrived at our destination. It was a beautiful fall day and the trees were full of color. The only problem was, we had absolutely nothing to talk about. I kept thinking, "Don't talk too much, you don't want to get on her nerves."

I have no idea what she was thinking. She initiated no conversation for the entire walk. I'm guessing she was as ready as I was for the hour to end. We simply didn't connect.

Don't beat your head against a brick wall trying to get someone who doesn't click with you to like you. If they don't, they don't. Move on.

It makes far better sense to invest your time and energy into individuals who give you a burst of renewed energy rather than to waste it on individuals who either can't, won't or don't support you.

> *There are seven billion people*
> *on the planet.*
> *Find the ones who like you.*

6. People willing to let you be you. Happy, healthy yeasayers pursuing their own dreams don't need or want to control you. Respect yourself enough to refuse to morph into someone you're not.

Seek out relationships with people who refrain from trying to fix, manipulate or manage you. When you surround yourself with individuals who aren't continually trying to change you, you'll be happier, they'll be happier, and you'll be free to create the best version of yourself.

7. Gentle truth tellers. Gentle truth tellers are individuals you can count on to be honest with you in a respectful manner. They let you know when you've messed up and hold you gently accountable for the way your behavior impacts them.

I'm blessed to have gentle truth tellers in my life, friends courageous enough to say, "Yeah, you do...," or "It frustrates me when you do this, I would prefer you..."

The truth isn't always easy to hear. Sometimes it's downright painful. On the flip side, truth prompts growth and allows you to make conscious choices.

> *Surround yourself with gentle truth tellers.*
> *You won't have to squander your energy walking*
> *on eggshells or trying to figure out what's wrong.*

Years ago, a close friend ditched me. Never willing to discuss things or try to mend our differences, all she would say was that she no longer wanted to be friends. I wept for days. I hurt for years.

She grossly underestimated who I was and how much I cared about her. Given a chance I would have changed my behaviors. Sadly, I was never given that chance.

As a result, I'm careful to look for truth tellers when cultivating new relationships. I also look for people who will work through problems with me and allow me the chance to grow and change.

If you are surrounded with supportive relationships, keep doing what you're doing. If you are isolated or investing in relationships with individuals who rob you of your energy and dull your dreams in the process, it's time to kick it up a notch.

Naysayers or Yeasayers

Pick to keep naysayers out of your inner circle.

Pick to surround yourself with supportive truth tellers.

Pick to savor the joy of successes shared.

Chapter 4

Inequitable or Even: Do Your Share

"Each person must be responsible for himself."

St. Paul

I once agreed to let someone live with me for three months. Not something I'd normally do, but it was short term, I had an available room and a colleague asked me to help.

The woman had been let go from her previous job, didn't have much money and lacked a support system. Having been greatly blessed, I believed I needed to bless others in return. I was happy to help.

In my effort to be helpful, I decided not to charge her rent. My thinking was that the money, while nice, wouldn't make all that much difference in my life. Having to pay it, on the other hand, would be a hardship for her.

Pick

Three months came and went. While she worked part-time at a grocery store, she hadn't found a full time job. I let her stay.

As the months dragged on I quickly shifted from being happy to help into feeling extremely frustrated and resentful. Despite knowing I was the one who had made the suggestion, it upset me that she never once offered to pay rent or help with utilities. It also bothered me that she wasn't actively looking for a job.

In addition, it drove me nuts that she was always home. When I left mid-morning, she was there. If I came home in the middle of the day, she was there. When I walked in after a long day's work, she was there.

I desperately wanted her to leave, but I felt trapped. She had nowhere to go, no one to help her.

As my frustrations grew, so did my complaints to everyone but her. Week after week I'd rant and rave. "Why doesn't she find a job?" "I can't even relax in my own home." "No one lives for free."

By month nine, I'd moved from anger to animosity. I was irate that she hadn't pursued getting a job, angry at God for not taking care of the situation and infuriated at myself for allowing her to move in in the first place.

Gathering all my courage I finally set a boundary, "In three months, job or not, I need you to move out." Having an end date helped me feel better. I'm sure you can imagine my relief when she was offered a great job across the state. My elation, however, was short lived.

"I turned them down," she informed me. "It's not what I want to do."

"Of course not," I thought. "You'd rather free load off me." Needless to say, I was infuriated, "Who in their right mind turns down a job in their field with a good salary and full benefits?" I complained to anyone who would listen.

As the "move out" date approached, she had nowhere to go. I couldn't win. If I kicked her out I was the bad guy, maybe even a bad person. If I let her stay, I'd seethe. Painful as it was, I opted to hold the boundary I'd set and insisted she leave.

She alternated between anger and angst. "You're selfish" and "You call yourself a Christian" were a few of the accusations she hurled at me. I would have preferred she say, "Thank you so much for your generosity and for all you've done for me."

While I found her anger disturbing, it was far easier to stomach than her painful, pitiful tears. As intended, her attempts to make me feel guilty hit the mark. Nevertheless, I gut-wrenchingly held my ground. While I hadn't minded helping her, I was no longer willing to take care of her.

It's hard enough to take care of myself.

Relief flooded me the day she left. I felt like I could breathe again. At the same time, I also felt sorrow for how things had turned out and for her. It's never easy to hold a boundary while watching someone stumble and suffer the consequences of their choices.

Struggling to get past my feelings of guilt, I examined how I, the one who'd helped her, became the "bad guy" in the equation. Despite her perception, I hadn't ruined her life.

Pick

I had simply stopped enabling her to mooch from me. Although it didn't feel like it, I'd done us both a huge favor.

That year was one of the most frustrating times of my life. It was also a time of great learning. It wasn't, however, until after she left that I fully recognized that when I choose to do more than my share, I enable someone to do less than their share.

Yes, you read that right. Every time I over-function, I enable someone to under-function.

Despite the fact I had acted out of kindness, I over-functioned when I provided rent free living for a capable, able-bodied adult. My actions enabled her to under-function for an entire year. If I hadn't insisted she leave, it would have been far longer.

Other examples of over-functioning enabling under-functioning include:

♦ Bailing out someone who has overspent.

♦ Calling in sick for a drunken spouse.

♦ Doing a coworker's tasks while they come in late, play on their computer or chitchat.

♦ Letting adult children live at home without helping out, contributing financially or actively looking for a job.

♦ Doing a child's homework or chores or not holding them accountable for getting things done in a timely manner. (Not to be confused with helping them with legitimate needs.)

Like many, I'm vulnerable to over-functioning when things aren't on my radar. In the case of my former roommate, I truly believed three months meant three months. It never occurred to me that she wouldn't actively look for work or would turn down a good job.

My friends and family were my frame of reference. Each of us would have done what it took to find a job. In fact, we would have gotten multiple jobs if needed in order to contribute financially. We wouldn't have been able to live with ourselves otherwise.

What I failed to realize is that people vary greatly in their frame of reference, character and upbringing. I can't assume that because I would or wouldn't do something that others operate from the same play book. Understanding this has freed me to recognize under-functioning far more quickly.

There are still times I over-function. When I do, my typical response is to lament, "I have no boundaries."

Elizabeth never fails to respond with, "Aw, pal, they flew in under your radar."

What a hopeful statement. Radars can be reset. I don't have to know everything and do everything right every time. I just need to be wise enough to learn and to reset my radar once I become aware.

Painful experiences produce wisdom.

The bottom line is, people with "sweet deals" aren't very motivated to move, grow or change. The woman I over-functioned for lived rent free in a beautiful home. She was safe and comfortable, why would she have been motivated to strike out on her own?

Instead of helping, over-functioning prevents others from maturing into responsible individuals capable of achieving hopes and dreams, having stellar careers and creating fulfilling relationships.

In addition, over-functioning weakens people and promotes unhealthy dependencies. Think of it like strength training. The more you exercise, the stronger you become. The more someone functions at an age-appropriate level, the stronger, more confident and capable they become.

It can be very difficult and painful to stop over-functioning. I, a therapist trained in setting boundaries, over-functioned for a stranger for almost an entire year before finally saying, "No more."

Stopping over-functioning for someone you dearly love such as a child, friend, sibling or parent is far more agonizing. Sadly, the only thing more excruciating than choosing to no longer over-function is the long term cost of under-functioning including broken relationships, depression and squandered lives.

When taken to extremes, kindness and compassion quickly become Achilles heels. While kindness and compassion are wonderful traits, the challenge is learning to balance them with fairness and accountability.

True kindness and compassion require holding others responsible for their choices.

Inequitable or Even

You are not a bad person for setting boundaries and refusing to over-function, even if you feel terrible doing so.

Repeat aloud, "I am not a bad person for setting boundaries and refusing to over-function" as often as needed for you to believe it.

It's as important to address under-functioning as it is over-functioning. Under-functioning includes letting others resolve problems, "mooching" and refusing to be "the bad guy." Under-functioning also entails doing less than one's fair share and abdicating personal responsibility for one's own happiness, time, finances, well-being and career.

I'm ashamed to admit it, but I have under-functioned and let others over-function for me. I've burned others by not completing my portion of assignments and letting them do the lion's share of the work. I've also let people who insisted on over-functioning do so. My mindset was, "If you really want to, great."

It meant I didn't have to. How wonderful for me.

Unfortunately, even with those who willingly over-functioned, my under-functioning created burdens, stress and resentment. It also left relationships strained, damaged or ruined beyond repair.

As I've grown healthier and recognize the impact of my behaviors on others, I try not to let others over-function for me. It's not fair, helpful or healthy, for me or for them.

While doing less than your share and under-functioning might sound tempting, it's helpful to consider its long-term consequences before you head off to find your own personal over-functioner.

Under-functioning:
+ Causes strife and resentment.
+ Kills love and respect.
+ Leads to broken relationships.
+ Creates burnout.
+ Squanders your talents and life.
+ Becomes a destructive, self-perpetuating pattern.

People under-function when they are enabled to do so. Reliant on over-functioners to take care of them, under-functioners find individuals willing to do more than their share. It's how they survive.

> *The best way to help an under-functioner is to quit over-functioning.*

When someone is no longer willing to over-function for them, the under-functioner:
+ Changes their behavior and accepts age appropriate responsibility.
+ Ups the ante, becoming aggressive or pitiful in an attempt to manipulate the over-functioner into continuing to do so.
+ Exits the system and finds a new over-functioner.

What about you, are your relationships lopsided? Do you ask others to do things you should be doing for yourself? Expect others to make exceptions? Take advantage of another's generosity? Do you regularly drop the ball, mooch or expect others to cover for you? Do you try to manipulate others into taking care of you?

Inequitable or Even

Or, are you an over-functioner? Is it hard for you to say no? Do you regularly do more than your share? Are you constantly being taken advantage of? Do you struggle with anger, resentment and bitterness? Are your dreams falling by the wayside because you're too busy over-functioning for others?

Whether your tendency is to over- or under-function, it's never too late to change. In choosing to do your share and asking others to do theirs, you set yourself and them up for success.

Guidelines for hitting equitable and even:

1. Ask yourself, "Boulder or Backpack?" Dr. John Townsend, in *Hiding From Love*, shares a metaphor I've used for nearly two decades as a guiding principle for determining when to help others. I love it because it takes emotion out of the decision and relieves my tendency to feel guilty.

Dividing life into boulders and backpacks, Townsend teaches we are obligated to help each other. At the same time, each person is personally responsible for their time, money, happiness, career and relationships.

Boulders are life's
crushing blows.

As caring, compassionate human beings, it's important to help when others are suffering from devastating events including death, divorce, illness, financial ruin or the loss of a job.

When a neighbor's child was diagnosed with cancer, a dear friend rallied help by letting others know there was a need. Some gave financial resources so they could hire someone to clean their house. Others watched the children. Still others provided meals.

Each act of generosity and help clearly stated, "You are not alone in your time of need."

My hope is that you'll always err on the side of helping those suffering tragedy and loss.

You'll feel good about lending a hand and they'll never forget your kindness. Additionally, when life deals you a crushing blow, you can expect what you have sown to come back to you.

Your backpack includes your job, happiness, the decisions you make and how you spend your time, money and resources.

> *Backpacks represent day-to-day living and the choices we make along the way.*

According to Townsend, those who under-function take their backpack off, plop down and wait for someone to come along and carry it for them. Once an over-functioner does, the under-functioner quickly learns it's nice to walk without the burden. Who can blame them? Hiking through life without a backpack is easier.

The problem with picking up another's backpack is that you inevitably exhaust yourself under the burden of their load in addition to your own.

Shortly after my freeloading roommate moved out, one of her acquaintances told me her sad tale of woe, "I'm quitting my job and won't be able to afford my place. I'm looking for somewhere to live." Then she paused, waiting for me to offer my vacant room.

"Unbelievable," I thought. "I'm a mark."

I'm not sure if under-functioners pass the word among themselves or if they can just smell an over-functioner a mile away. Either way, they find over-functioners easier than kids find candy.

Wiser because of what had happened previously and armed with Townsend's boulder/backpack question, I recognized her request. Biting my tongue I silently declined to become her sherpa.

Thankfully, I had learned from the previous lesson and didn't need another painful experience to acquire wisdom.

Be quick to help those crushed by life's unexpected blows, but refuse to over-function.

2. Guilt goes away. Guilt at saying no to over-functioning goes away. You may doubt yourself; that's ok. You may think you're being selfish; you're not. You may feel terrible; it will pass. Grit your teeth if you must, but don't give in to the temptation to over-function.

Inappropriate guilt goes away. For me it generally takes anywhere from 15 minutes to two days. Resentment on the other hand builds, steals your joy and the resources you need in order to create a life you love and achieve your own hopes and dreams.

Pick

You can greatly speed up getting rid of guilt feelings by considering how the under-functioner should be responding. Framing under-functioning behavior with what would be more acceptable greatly lessens guilt.

An individual who lives rent free should be tripping over themself to say thanks and to help out. A person who doesn't contribute shouldn't get credit for doing so. Someone who borrows money should be paying it back, not avoiding payment or asking for more.

3. Gently and firmly, without apology, hold others accountable for their behavior. While it's hard to let others figure things out for themselves and to see them suffer the consequences of their choices, it's actually a gift. It just doesn't feel like one at the time. Having to live with the consequences of choices is what most motivates change.

For example, while I'd prefer you not tell my mother, I've been pulled over more than once for speeding. Most of the officers took pity on me and, instead of giving me the ticket I deserved, let me off with a warning. Appreciative and anxious to be on my way, I'd get back on the road and roar away with a smile.

No such luck the last time I got pulled over. I was coming around a bend, going too fast and was caught. No argument. No mercy. The officer simply handed me the ticket and told me to slow down. The fine was $185, plus points on my license. Writing that check to the state was painful.

I learned more from having to pay that ticket than from all the warnings combined. Specifically, I learned that appropriate boundaries modify behavior. I prefer to spend

48

my money on things I need and want. Being forced to spend my savings on a speeding ticket not only got my attention, it also significantly modified my behavior. I slowed down.

While I appreciated the warnings, the painful punishment of parting with my money was far more effective and lasting.

Consequences
create change.

While over-functioning may solve an immediate problem, it creates more problems in the long run. Yes, you may meet a critical deadline or get things done without a fight, but over-functioning sets you up to continue to do more than your share.

You'll never have the life you desire or were designed to live if you over-function. You alone are responsible for protecting your resources and setting yourself up for success. Next time you're tempted to over-function, just say no.

Conversely, you can't reap the rewards of a well-lived life if you don't step up and do your share. Each time you take responsibility for your life, you set yourself up for success.

Pick to treat and be treated fairly.

Pick boulders not backpacks.

Pick more productivity, more peace and more passion.

Chapter 5

Tolerate or Terminate: Banish Bad Behavior

"Why do so many people let their dreams die unlived? The biggest reason, I suppose is the negative, cynical attitudes of other people."

Og Mandino

I'll never forget the first time I gave a speech. It was my freshman year in high school and I was nervous beyond belief. With great trepidation, I walked to the front of the room knowing I'd rather have a root canal than be speaking center stage.

Having rehearsed many times, I started into my three minute talk. With my voice and knees shaking like leaves in the autumn wind, I kept it together for about 30 seconds.

Pick

Then, my nervousness took over and I got the giggles. Horrified, I tried to stop laughing, but I could only get a few words out between giggles. I was too nervous.

"Sit down and take an F," boomed the teacher.

Stunned silence filled the room.

Shocked and sobered, I took my seat. Shame coursed through my body. Humiliation heated my face. I hunched down hoping to hide. Silent tears slid down my cheeks. Degraded and embarrassed, I felt rage race through me.

As I write and relive that moment, my chest still constricts and tears flow anew. Young, insecure and shy, I was publicly disgraced. While other childhood memories have long been forgotten, that one is still seared into my brain. It's ironic that I became a professional speaker.

I never said a word to the teacher about how he treated me that day. I hadn't yet found my voice. If I knew then what I know now, I would have called him on his bad behavior. Humiliating another human being is reprehensible. Regardless of whether my giggles were annoying, I deserved to be treated with dignity and respect.

I wonder just how many students he wounded with caustic remarks. I seriously doubt I was the first, and I certainly wasn't the last. Bad behavior left unchecked grows.

While I didn't have the knowledge or the courage to confront a teacher at the time, I've long since learned to advocate for myself and hold people gently accountable for how their behavior impacts me. I've also learned to set appropriate boundaries that enable me to keep safe distances from unsafe individuals.

Tolerate or Terminate

What about you? Do you find yourself on the receiving end of cutting comments? Are you able to stand up for yourself in the face of bad behavior? Or do you slip away silently, losing a bit of your shine and joy each time it happens?

Do you have a hard time setting boundaries? Do you even know what a boundary is?

Whether you've tried to set boundaries before and failed miserably, you're hearing the term boundaries for the first time, or you're setting appropriate boundaries on a regular basis, you must identify and mitigate bad behaviors if you want to create a life you love.

The following will help you identify destructive behaviors and set boundaries that help bring about lasting change:

1. **Tell yourself the truth about the behaviors of the people in your life as well as your own.** While you might not like what you see, telling yourself the truth is the first step to setting boundaries and changing your life for the better.

2. **Banish bad behavior through boundaries.** Gators, takers, drainers, liars and players will siphon away time, resources and joy. Unless you set and hold appropriate boundaries with each of these, they will divert precious resources and derail your dreams.

Gators — Gators, like the alligators they are, lie in wait then pounce unexpectedly. Like my former speech teacher, they can take a hunk of your soul in their attack.

Pick

Gators generally start small, taking jabs under the guise of humor. When you have the audacity to call them on their bad behavior, they tell you, "Get a sense of humor."

In mild forms, gators simply throw covert jabs. Unfortunately, just as alligators in the wild grow larger over time, gators left unchecked become increasingly unsafe and can escalate into verbal, emotional and physical abusers.

There's a reason alligators haven't replaced dogs as man's best friend. They aren't safe to be around. Yet, far too many people give gators free access to their lives, hopes and dreams. The following tips will help you recognize and back down gators:

♦ **Call gators on their behavior.** My first year in a new job, one of my coworkers took a jab at me in a meeting. I went to her office afterwards and asked, "Are you angry at me or have I done something to offend you?"

"No, no," she assured me. "I'm just under a lot of stress."

"Well, if I do something that frustrates you, please let me know. In the meantime, I'd prefer you not take jabs at me." I replied gently calling her on her bad behavior.

No jabs occurred for one year.

The following year, we had the exact same conversation. No jabs for another year.

The third year, you guessed it, the exact same behavior and the exact same chat took place. Only that time I ended my portion of the conversation with, "I'm wondering what we need to do so that we don't have to have this conversation next year."

No jabs for 12 years.

Because I addressed her gator bites respectfully each and every time they occurred, my coworker's bad behavior never escalated.

When you encounter gator behavior, have the conversation and hold the boundary each and every time the behavior occurs.

> *The secret to keeping gators small is to nip bad behavior in the bud each and every time it occurs.*

♦ **Put as much distance between yourself and a gator as possible.** If you've confronted a gator's bad behavior and they aren't ready, willing or able to make changes, you need to set and maintain boundaries.

Depending on the situation, appropriate boundaries may include limiting your interactions with them, curtailing what you're willing to talk with them about or only engaging in conversations when a powerful third party is present.

♦ **Get to a good counselor if you're in an abusive relationship.** Once a pattern of abuse has been established, it generally takes professional help to break the destructive cycle. The larger the gator, the more outside assistance is needed as gators are brilliant at turning the tables and blaming their victims for their behaviors.

Pick

Takers — Takers, like my former roommate, are individuals who chronically under-function in relationships by taking another's resources, time and talent while giving little, if anything, back. A taker's first priority is to meet their own needs. Unfortunately, they meet those needs at the expense of others.

In healthy relationships, both parties give and take and no one's resources and good will become strained. Takers, as their name implies, take far more than they give in relationships.

Taking can emerge in many forms, but the commonality is that takers take everything you'll give them including your time, energy, resources, possessions, generosity and good will. Then, they take even more. Rarely do they give anything in return.

For example, many takers talk on and on about their problems and what's going wrong in their life. Unfortunately, when you happen to need a sympathetic ear, takers quickly disappear. Or, they hijack conversations back with a, "I know what you mean. Just last week I…"

Takers also have a nasty habit of relying on others to over-function for them at home and in the workplace. In other words, they sponge off others. Takers also let others do far more than their share of work. Especially infuriating are the times a taker takes credit for a project to which they contributed little.

Takers also tend to let others do the lion's share of the work in relationships. If you're in a relationship where you're the one who does all the initiating, you're probably in a relationship with a taker. While that doesn't make them a bad person, it does indicate that they aren't doing their fair share of the work to keep a relationship strong.

Takers can also be "borrowers." Unfortunately, they don't tend to take care of or return what they've borrowed.

I once made the mistake of lending a taker I'd just met $250 dollars. Through tears she'd shared her compelling story with me, "My family's having money problems. I just need it to get through the month. I'll pay you back $25 a month starting next month. I promise."

More than 15 years have come and gone since I naively wrote that check. She never made a single payment. It infuriated me for years that she felt it was okay to take my hard earned money. Not wanting to stay trapped in anger, I finally chose to be grateful to have learned my lesson at $250 rather than at a greater amount.

If you make the mistake of lending money to a taker, kiss it goodbye.

In short, takers under-function in many areas of their lives and tend to view anyone who's willing to over-function for them as fair game.

Unless you have good boundaries including valuing yourself as well as others and saying no to bad behavior, your hard work and generosity enable takers to enjoy the exact same benefits you have earned as a hard and loyal worker.

♦ **Expect reciprocity in relationships.** I'm not saying you should expect everything to be 50-50 all the time. At the same time, if you're the one who's doing the lion's share of the giving in a relationship, value yourself enough to engage in give and take.

> *Healthy relationships balance giving and taking.*

♦ **Don't lend money to takers.** If you want to give someone money and you have the resources to do it without jeopardizing yourself or your family's future, give it outright. Otherwise keep your money in your pocket.

My father recently told me of a man who's asked him for money multiple times. Dad set a clear boundary with the man. "I'll lend you $20 dollars. If you pay me back, you'll show me you can be trusted." The man took the twenty, but never paid him back. My father was far wiser than I was with my taker.

♦ **Refuse to over-function for others.** As discussed in the previous chapter, help those in need from life's crippling blows. At the same time, remember that each person is responsible for his or her own happiness, time, resources, job and well-being.

Drainers – Drainers often to have chaotic, traumatic and difficult lives. Carrying a great deal of pain, frustration and disappointment they tend to go through life depressed and defeated with a gray cloud hovering over their heads. They have an uncanny ability to immediately suck the life out of any room and individual in their presence.

While life has handed them tough circumstances, drainers sadly contribute to their own unhappiness and the chaos of their lives by under-functioning. In their pain they indiscriminately share too much information about the intimate details of their lives. Drainers also tend to attach themselves to anyone willing to help or listen.

Sadly, their under-functioning and dependency on others causes drainers to quickly burn through their support systems. In addition, they eventually frustrate anyone who tries to give them advice as they come up with a myriad of reasons why offered solutions won't work.

I hope that you will always treat drainers with great kindness, respect and compassion. At the same time I urge you to remember that each person, yourself included, is responsible for their own life and for working through their own pains, failures and disappointments.

♦ **Limit how much time you devote to drainers.** Instead of spending hour after hour with a drainer, limit your time to what you can do cheerfully. For me that's usually 10 to 30 minutes.

♦ **Develop an exit strategy.** Knowing that it usually takes North Americans three to four verbal cues such as "I've got to get going" before a conversation comes to a close, I start conversations with drainers with "I only have a few minutes."

If they are talking incessantly, I interrupt them several times saying, "I really do have to get going."

Pick

When they don't get the message—and drainers typically don't—I apologize, say goodbye and get going.

♦ **Don't throw your pearls to pigs.** A key characteristic of a drainer is that they don't put advice into action. Dave, a friend who has helped countless college students, has one rule: "If you're not going to do something differently, I'm not going to let you waste my time having the same conversation over and over."

♦ **Refer drainers to someone whose life mission is to help others turn their lives around.** If you don't, they will run you ragged, devour precious energy and resources, and leave you depleted and defeated.

> *Don't let drainers drain*
> *and drag you down.*

Liars – Liars, people who chronically cause you to doubt yourself and what truth is, drain your energy, and waste your time sending you on wild goose chases. If you want to create a life you love, you can't squander your resources on liars.

It's a very rare individual who doesn't tell a lie on occasion. Whoppers have certainly come out of my mouth. The difference between a liar and one who's not is whether or not they go back and set the record straight.

♦ **Tell yourself the truth.** Recognize liars for who they are and for what they can and can't do. If you suspect someone is a liar, don't fully trust them unless and until you see sustained behavior changes over a long span of time.

♦ **Call them on their lies.** Allowing lies emboldens a liar to tell more lies. Gently call them on their lie. They may not change their story, but both of you will know the truth.

♦ **Set boundaries.** Give liars as little access to your life as possible. You'll be happier and have to spend far less energy determining what the truth is.

Players – Similar to liars, players hold out hope or make implied or stated promises, but repeatedly fail to follow through on their promises.

Players can be parents, dates, spouses, co-workers and just about anyone you meet. While not always the case, they tend to be charming, attractive and fun. In fact, players are often life's "golden boys or girls."

Players possess an impeccable sense of knowing when others are becoming fed up with them and are unwilling to tolerate their bad behavior any longer. When they see you getting ready to say, "Enough already," they'll toss you a bone in order to keep you under their spell for a while longer.

> *Players hold out the hope, but only give you enough to keep you in their orbit.*

Long ago, I had started working on a different book with a very nice man. I was flattered and excited that he wanted to work with me. Each time we met, he promised he'd get something done. It took me three meetings before I awoke to the fact that while he talked a great game, he never produced any writing.

Knowing I'd go ballistic if we hit the big time and he took credit for the book in an interview on national television, I recognized I needed to talk to him and give him a chance to produce. He was deeply hurt and offended at my insinuation that he hadn't produced any written work. He again promised to have something for the next time we met.

We met again, and true to form, he still hadn't written anything. It was at that point we decided to go our separate ways with him retaining the right to use whatever he had written and me retaining the right to use whatever I produced. It was tough, but because we'd had an honest conversation, our friendship remained intact.

♦ **Recognize players for who they are and for what they can and cannot do.** If you're constantly being hurt or left waiting for someone to do something, tell yourself the truth. If a person never shows up or only gives you a fraction of their attention when they do, they are a player.

♦ **If you're involved with a player, gently but honestly tell them how their behavior impacts you and ask specifically for what you need.** If they can follow through on their promises, great. If they can't, move on and find someone who is ready, willing and able to engage in a healthy, reciprocal relationship with you.

♦ **Regularly remind yourself that you are worth more than the measly crumbs a player tosses**

your way. You deserve to be an honored guest feasting at the banquet table, not a beggar thankful for tiny crumbs. You sell yourself short of what you deserve when you decide to get by on table scraps.

A player's behavior isn't a reflection of your worth as a person. It's a reflection of their mental health and how little others have required of them in previous relationships.

Roses – At the end of the day, Dee Brestin, author of *The Friendships of Women* reminds readers that the price of every relationship, even with a healthy individual, is similar to the price of a rose: beauty accompanied by thorns. Bumping into an occasional thorn is inevitable in any relationship that has depth and duration.

The truth of the matter is, everyone will eventually hurt or let you down to some degree. It's part of being a flawed human being. The trick is to learn to let healthy people in, while screening out unhealthy and unsafe individuals.

It is wisest to avoid individuals who willingly, for whatever reason, cause pain and damage to another's soul.

If you want to create a life you love, recognize people for who they are and for what they can and can't do. Set and lovingly hold boundaries with gators, takers, drainers, liars and players. Fail to do so and you'll squander away your ability to live life to the fullest and accomplish your dreams.

Pick

Pick to be wise.

Pick to protect precious resources.

Pick to banish bad behaviors.

Chapter 6

Give or Guard: When and How To Say No

"Learn to say 'no.' It will be far more useful than Latin, algebra or anything else you'll learn in college."
Dr. Charles Swindoll

I have a bright, shiny orange lawnmower in my garage, not an unusual place to keep one. What isn't readily apparent is the fact that when I bought it I didn't need a lawnmower, I didn't want a lawnmower and I didn't plan on using the lawnmower. I had a lawn service.

Why on earth would I buy something I didn't need, want or plan to use? Because, even though I've been working on it for over two decades, there are still times I struggle with saying one very simple, ever so tiny, powerful word: No.

65

Pick

Here's the back story. I'd hired a good friend's son to mow my lawn. Great. He had a lawnmower. Even better. I was happy to pay him to put it to use.

One day, for whatever reason, he decided to use my old mower instead of his nicer, newer model. My mower slowly sputtered to life, resentful to be awakened from its silent slumber. It worked, but it wasn't pretty.

Straining and struggling, he pushed and shoved the protesting mower across the bumpy yard. Smoke billowed out, coating the grass with a low lying cloud. He wasn't happy. Neither was the machine.

His father called me the next day, "Sherene, no pressure, but if you want a lawnmower, I can help you. I know the guys at the hardware store and they can set you up with a good one."

He handed me the perfect out. I could have said no. I wanted to say no. I should have said no. What came out of my mouth was, "That would be great, thanks."

Several days later he called me back. "I found a good mower for you. It's $275. I had them set it aside for you if you want it, all you have to do is give them a call. No pressure."

Gentleman that he was, he once again handed me the perfect out. I, once again, blew it.

"Thanks, I really appreciate your help. I'll pick it up tomorrow."

I drove to the store knowing I didn't want the mower. I politely purchased the machine knowing I didn't want it. I even thanked the man for selling me the unwanted machine.

To this day, that mower sits in my garage, a silent sentinel that reminds me multiple times a day of the importance of saying no.

What did I learn from buying a machine I never wanted or needed? Beyond the fact that I obviously needed to tighten my boundaries and get better at saying no, I also learned that people have a right to both ask for and offer things. It's my job to determine what works for me.

In an ideal world, I'd never have to say no. I don't, however, live in an ideal world. People will be asking for and offering me things for the rest of my life. I need to expect it, be able to determine what works for me and say no to the things for which I have neither interest, need nor resources.

I am responsible for being honest with myself and others about what I do and don't want. I need to get over trying to ensure everyone likes me and approves of everything I do. Even after all these years, I still find myself wanting two things: to look good and for everyone to be happy.

Saying no is critical to creating a happy, productive life. The better I get at saying no, the more assets I have to devote to my dreams and to the things that truly matter.

People don't have to like hearing my no. I certainly don't like it when others turn me down. However, no is a part of healthy relationships and healthy individuals are accepting of another's no.

An indicator of good mental health is the willingness to accept another's no.

67

Pick

When I say yes when I want and need to say no, resentment and regret begin to squeeze my neck, choke my breathing and slowly settle into my chest. Resentment's heaviness lingers longer with every unwanted yes I utter.

I have far too many hopes and dreams to accomplish. I simply can't afford to have resentment and regret stealing my joy and holding me back.

The bottom line is, I get mad when I say yes when I want to say no. While I initially think I'm mad at the person for asking, I've found I'm really mad at myself for not having better boundaries and protecting precious assets including my joy, time, energy and money.

If I can't do something cheerfully, I need to say no. Doing so protects me. It also protects the relationship and the other person.

At the end of the day, instead of viewing no as negative, I find it helpful to remember that a no to something good is a yes to something better. For example, a no to a lawnmower I didn't need would have been a yes to my hot tub fund. Additionally:

- A no to overworking is a yes to relationships.
- A no to overspending is a yes to financial freedom.
- A no to distractions is a yes to my dreams.

What about you? Do you find yourself buying or accepting things from others you don't need or want? Do you find yourself saying yes to things you don't need or want to do? Does the very thought of making waves unsettle you? Do you think saying no to a request makes you selfish? Do you worry others won't like you if you tell them no?

Do you want to learn how and when to say no? Do you want to achieve your dreams? Do you want healthier relationships and a happier life?

The following will help empower and equip you to say no professionally and personally to things you don't need or want, to things that are bad for you and to things for which you have neither the time nor resources.

Knowing when to say no professionally can be tricky, particularly in today's uncertain world. Ask yourself the following questions to help ensure you have the time and energy needed to do your job well, to prevent burnout and to minimize the resentment that accompanies overfunctioning in the workplace:

1. **If your answers to the following questions are no, let additional work tasks go.**

♦ **Am I the only one who can do this?** If you are the only one with the expertise or time, take on the extra task and do it with excellence. You'll increase your value, enhance your reputation and help your organization.

♦ **Will doing this help me achieve my dreams?** If an opportunity will help you get where you want to go and you have the time, energy and reserves, go for it. Strategically saying yes to key opportunities opens doors and positions you for future success.

♦ **Is this a bona fide emergency?** There are times when it's vital for all hands to be on deck. If the request is one of those times, pitch in and be a team player.

Pick

Allowing someone to do less than their share—to underfunction—is an entirely different matter. If you repeatedly bail another person out by doing their tasks, you'll be resentful and your work and attitude will suffer. Worse yet, you teach them it's okay to slack off and that you'll do their work. How wonderful for them.

The bottom line is if you want healthier relationships and a happier life, you can't afford to do another's job in addition to your own. Unless it's a bona fide emergency, politely decline the request.

While it's difficult to say no to professional requests, it can be even harder to say no to family and friends. Knowing when to say no empowers you to protect important relationships and the resources you need to create a life you love.

2. **Use the following questions to help you determine when to decline personal requests.**

♦ **Do I have the resources?** Living beyond your means financially, emotionally or physically can delay or even derail the fulfillment of your dreams. If your answer is no, definitely let it go.

♦ **Does it fit with my short and long term goals?** If you want to create a life you love, you need to keep focused on what truly matters. Say no to the things that divert your time, talent and treasure from your priorities.

♦ **Can I do it cheerfully?** Saying yes to things you don't want to do invites resentment and ruins relationships. I've been on the receiving and giving end of begrudged help. Both left a terrible taste in my mouth. If you can't do something cheerfully, answer no and let it go.

Recognizing when to say no is a terrific starting point. Equally important is knowing *how* to say no. I've learned a lot from my dear friend, Nancy, who's great at saying no. She's kind and firm and keeps her statements straightforward and simple.

When she turns me down she simply says, "That doesn't work for me, pal." No explanation. No groveling. No trying to convince me she still cares about me. In response I don't argue with her or think she doesn't like me. I simply accept her no and we work out something else. How simple is that?

I, on the other hand, still fight against wishy-washy, verbal diarrhea when I say no.

Yes, you read that right.

My natural tendency is to tell all the reasons *why* I can't do something in a voice as lacking conviction and power as a wet noodle. "I'd love to help you, but I really don't have the time. I'm working hard to finish my book and it's taking a lot of energy. I really would like to help, but I just can't. Do you hate me?"

Just yesterday I fought, and I'm happy to report overcame, the urge to give multiple explanations while turning down a request. Every time I win this battle I feel better about myself. An added bonus is that I get far fewer requests to change my mind. It's amazing.

Pick

3. Use the following "go to" phrases for saying no like a pro:

♦ **"No."** It's a complete response.

♦ **"No, thank you."** A polite, albeit short response.

♦ **"That doesn't work for me."** I love Nancy's go to response. I just drop off the "pal." Add it back if it works for you.

♦ **"Thanks for thinking of me. I'm flattered, but I need to say no."** Polite and honoring.

♦ **"I can't, but thanks for asking."** Short, simple, straightforward.

♦ **"While I can't do <u>xyz</u>, I'd be happy to do <u>abc</u>."** A win-win for both parties.

♦ **"What would work better for me is . . ."** Allows you to negotiate what you can do cheerfully.

♦ **"Let me get back with you."** As a person who gets excited about opportunities and quickly says yes, this line is one of my favorites. It gets me away from the heat of the moment and allows me to consider my schedule and resources before I take on another commitment.

While saying no may never be effortless, it does get easier. Say no regularly and you'll be happier, more productive and far less stressed. Be patient with yourself as you learn to say no. You'll get better and better at telling yourself the truth about what you do and don't want to do and protecting your limited time and resources.

*Wisdom is acquired each time you
learn from your mistakes.
Be nice to yourself as you grow.*

Lastly, anticipate resistance when you start saying no. Expect begging, pleading, bullying and the silent treatment. You might even lose a few unhealthy, lopsided relationships along the way.

"Why?" you ask.

People have a vested interest in your continuing to say yes. It works for them. But that doesn't mean it's good for you, your family or your dreams.

As a person desiring healthier relationships and a happier life, you must protect your time, talent and resources. Your ability to say no significantly impacts whether you'll live your dreams or watch them fall by the wayside.

Pick to protect precious resources.

Pick to say no.

Pick to be powerful.

Chapter 7
Chaotic or Conducive: Conquer Clutter

"A duty dodged is like a debt unpaid: it is only deferred, and we must come back and settle the account at last."

Joseph F. Newton

I t started innocently enough. I had several "left over" boxes from my move. They held stuff I wasn't willing to part with, but didn't need for day-to-day living and things I promised myself I'd organize once I got settled.

Consumed with starting a new job, I pushed the extra boxes into a room and closed the door. Out of sight, out of mind, they were easy to ignore.

In the months that followed, whenever I didn't know what to do with something I threw it in the room. Like rabbits, my mess multiplied quickly. Boxes and bags piled

75

upon each other. Loose papers were strewn everywhere. I was embarrassed, I looked like a hoarder. Even worse, I couldn't find anything when I needed it.

Mom came to visit the first summer. Knowing she was a good organizer, loved me and would want to help, I innocently asked, "Momma, will you help me de-clutter the front room?"

Her big blue eyes grew bigger, but her reply was simply, "Yes, dear."

For an entire week as I headed off to teach, she entered the war zone. Upon my return she daily greeted me with three piles: Things she thought I should keep; things to get rid of and things she wasn't sure about. We'd weed through the piles and put away the things I was keeping.

We rewarded ourselves by going out to dinner. It never hurts to keep helpers happy.

If you're like me, one job always leads to another. Mom was doing so great, I also asked her to help me with my bedroom closet. Long and narrow, it held a lot. Unfortunately, I couldn't step inside more than a foot because my things were strewn everywhere.

Without complaint, Mom slaved away until it was cleared of clutter. I squealed with delight.

Equally exciting, Mom finished the front room the last day of her visit. Happy as a clam, I gave her a huge hug.

Her response, forever seared in my memory, was far less enthusiastic. She simply looked at me, eyes filling with tears and took a long, ragged breath.

In my "it's all about me" world, I hadn't considered the burden I'd placed on her by under-functioning and asking her to take care of my messes. All I can say is it's a good thing she loves me.

Nearly 20 years have come and gone since I pushed my mother near the breaking point. While I still have a tendency to pile things up when I get too tired or busy, I'm happy to report I've kept the clutter beast at bay. Thanks to Mom, I haven't filled up a room or closet since.

Mom skillfully moved me from cluttered and chaotic to calm and conducive. In doing so she taught me multiple things, first and foremost, clutter causes anxiety.

I knew the clutter bothered me, but it wasn't until it was gone that I discovered its impact. Instead of being anxious and having a job hanging over my head, I experienced peace. My house became a sanctuary where I could rest and restore after a hard day's work.

Clutter also creates chaos and wastes valuable time. In addition to living with the cluttered closet and junk room I drove a messy car, lost valuable documents, failed to cash checks and routinely hunted for my keys. Stress and mini-crises were regular occurrences. Thanks to Mom, I no longer squander precious time and energy searching for things.

Clutter additionally reduces productivity and saps away energy, focus and creativity. Now that my world is organized, I'm able to devote my attention to what matters most, be it pursuing dreams, investing in relationships or doing something fun. I'm free.

Pick

Clutter also multiplies quickly. Putting off taking care of things by promising myself, "I'll do it later," created a breeding ground for clutter to accumulate. A task that if handled immediately would have only taken minutes can quickly balloon into hours, days or even weeks.

Lastly, physical clutter is a manifestation of emotional clutter. I've yet to meet anyone who lives in physical clutter who doesn't have an emotionally cluttered life. While it may be hard to hear, the truth is that clutter and chaos go hand in hand.

When I wrote this chapter I proudly declared, "It's been almost 20 years since Mom helped me out. I'm happy to report I've tamed the clutter beast."

True at the time, clutter recently began to creep back into my life. As I write, there are multiple, albeit it small, piles in my office and closet. Knowing that physical clutter is a manifestation of emotional clutter you're probably wondering, "What's going on?"

Well, in the midst of transitioning jobs and finishing *Pick*, I let things pile up. While I've started to tackle what I've let accumulate, I'm not yet done. As my soul craves a peaceful environment and clutter makes me shudder, my commitment to you is to get the piles put away.

What about you? Is clutter weighing you down? Do you live in a world of "I'll do it tomorrow?"

Are your closets and drawers overflowing? Is your house a mess? Are you too embarrassed to have company? What about your car? Do you cringe when you have to give someone a ride? Do you regularly waste time hunting for keys, bills and things you need? Do you long for a peaceful environment and a life free of chaos and clutter?

> *If you spend even five minutes a day looking for things, in a year you'll have wasted almost four full work days.*

Getting organized can feel overwhelming, especially if you think you're going to have to spend all day, week or month working on it. The following are tips my mother taught me for overcoming clutter:

1. De-clutter in short blocks of time. Devote short blocks of time to a specific project. For example, carve out anywhere from 15 minutes to three hours to attack the clutter in your kitchen.

Unless you're getting ready to put your house on the market next week, doing multiple projects and working on clutter for over three hours at a time is a setup for burnout. Trying to tackle too much too quickly only ensures it will be a long time before you muster the energy to attack your clutter again.

Even if you are totally gung-ho to get your clutter under control, don't overdo it. Clutter accumulates over time. Set yourself up for success by tackling your messes in short segments.

2. Divide clutter into piles. To weed through clutter quickly, divide things into four piles.

Pick

- *Keep it* – Put the things you know you want to keep in one pile. At the end of your de-clutter session, put them away.

- *Toss it* – Throw away things that you don't need or want and that can't be used by others. For example, useless paper, isolated bits and pieces, things that are broken...

- *Give it away/sell it* – If you want to make money from your castoffs, have a garage sale or take gently used items to a consignment shop.

    If the thought of having a garage sale makes you slightly nauseous, get a tax write off by giving things you no longer need or use to a charitable organization such as Goodwill or Salvation Army.

> *One man's junk is another*
> *man's treasure.*

    If you're still reluctant to part with things because you might need or want them someday, tell yourself the truth by asking questions such as: When was the last time I used it? Do I really need it? Does it fit? What's the worst thing that could happen if I toss it? Can someone else use it?

- *Not certain what to do with it* – While the "keep it" and "toss it" piles are relatively easy, if you're anything like me, you have things you're not certain about. The last thing you want to do while de-cluttering is to get bogged down in decision making.

Throw everything you can't make an easy decision about into your "not certain" pile. At the end of each session, revisit the "not certain" pile and make your decisions. I find it helpful to remember that it's possible to have too much and that the things I give away can be used to bless others.

3. **Everything needs a home.** When my mom cleared my clutter she repeatedly said, "Everything needs a home." We bought and built bookshelves, purchased umpteen tubs and made a specific place for everything I owned.

As usual, Mom was right. When things have a home, it's easy to put them away. When they don't, they pile up or get moved back and forth from one place to another.

Depending on what you're de-cluttering, you're going to need:

♦ Shelving

♦ Tubs

♦ A file cabinet or storage bin

♦ Files

If mom had just helped me de-clutter, my mess would have returned. Because she ensured everything had a home, I've kept things up. Thanks Mom.

4. **Enlist the help of others.** Mom, Dad and some friends helped me tackle the clutter in my garage by building a cabinet and several storage units. Add in two wide shelves, 12 tubs and considerable elbow grease and my garage was transformed. Best of all, I can find anything I need in less than a minute.

Pick

It's far easier to de-clutter with the help of someone else. If you make it fun, keep it simple, act appreciative and help others in return, people are generally more than willing to help you.

> *It's far easier to de-clutter*
> *with the help of someone else.*

Get your kids and spouse in on the act or trade decluttering days with a friend. If you can afford it, pay a store to build and deliver shelving. Even better, hire a professional organizer who will happily help you tackle your clutter.

5. Become a "do it now" person. The last tip for overcoming clutter is to deal with it daily. Instead of saying, "I'll do it tomorrow," tell yourself the truth. Tomorrow rarely, if ever, comes. A job like sorting the mail takes less than five minutes and little energy the day it arrives. Let it pile up and you can spend hours getting it back under control.

> *Keeping ahead of clutter is*
> *the best line of defense.*

Keep clutter at bay by handling everyday matters every day. Quick tips include:

♦ *Mail –* Toss the junk, shred things that can lead to a stolen identity and put your bills and important papers into appropriate files.

I keep four files at my mail sorting spot— bills, personal, business and medical. Since adopting this system, I've never lost important information. Additionally, preparing my taxes is far easier because everything I need is in one easily accessible place.

* **Car** – Throw out trash as soon as you get home and immediately put away anything you were transporting. If you have kids, keep their toys in a small tub.

* **Clothing** – Immediately hang your clothes up or put them in the hamper. Having a centralized family hamper or one in each bedroom closet helps tremendously.

* **Toys** – Train your children to put their toys away before they get out more, and make sure they put them away at the end of every day. If it's a battle, make it a game. Kids love competing to see who can pick up the most the quickest.

* **Dishes** – At the end of every meal or before you go to bed at night, tidy up your kitchen and dining area. Empty the dishwasher or drying rack as soon as your dishes are done and you'll always have a place for the next set of dirty dishes. One other tip, rinse dishes as soon as you use them. They come clean with little effort. Waiting ensures you'll spend far more time and elbow grease.

* **Magazines** Read and recycle, and don't renew subscriptions unless you actually read them.

While it may seem easiest in the short run to let things pile up, a cluttered office, house or car takes its toll. Keeping your space clutter-free goes a long ways towards creating an environment where your creativity and dreams can flourish.

Pick

Pick to overcome chaos and clutter.
Pick to stay on top of things.
Pick to create a conducive environment.

Chapter 8

Miserable or Marvelous: Keep a Clean Plate

"Live so you wouldn't be ashamed to sell
the family parrot to the town gossip."
Will Rogers

C linical supervision. Two words that strike fear in the heart of counseling students. I had just started my doctoral program, was working hard and wanted the faculty to think they'd made a good decision admitting me. Entering my session, I braced myself for the critical feedback sure to follow.

Dr. Freeman began by asking me, "Did you review your tapes?"

"Yes," I assured her.

"Then let's get to work," she replied.

Pick

The hour passed quickly.

"Thanks, Dr. Freeman." I said heading out the door. "I appreciate your help."

I almost made it to the exit before my appropriately guilty conscience kicked in. I had lied about watching my tapes. Guilt washed over me. My stomach sickened.

"It's just a little white lie." I rationalized. "She'll never know. I'll view them from now on."

Sounded like a good plan to me. The problem was the part of me that loves the freedom and peace that accompanies living guilt-free knew my guilt wouldn't go away on its own. I would only be able to push it aside.

I faced a critical juncture: live with the guilt or go back, fess up and face the consequences. It wasn't an easy choice.

Shuffling slowly, I headed back to Dr. Freeman's office. I didn't want to face the embarrassment or the potential punishment I might receive once I told the truth.

"What if she hates me? Will she kick me out of the program? Why didn't I just tell the truth in the first place?"

With high anxiety, I reluctantly knocked on her door.

Glancing up, she queried, "Yes?"

"Um," I hemmed, mortified to the core.

"I just lied to you," I blurted out. "I didn't watch my tapes. I'm sorry."

"Okay," she said slowly. "Why did you lie?"

"Because I wanted to look better in your eyes."

"I'd prefer you not do that in the future," she replied.

"Me too," I agreed. "I don't ever want to have to repeat this conversation."

Leaving her office, lightheartedness replaced my mortification and guilt. I was free to live fully in the present without having to push down or cover up any guilt, shame or secrets. My plate was clean.

I learned a great deal from that experience including I prefer to not mess up in the first place. Had I simply done my assignment, the entire saga would have been avoided. When I'm wise, I do the right thing. Unfortunately, I'm not always wise, and messing up is part of the human condition.

I also learned that when I mess up, it's better to fess up and face the music than it is to make things worse by lying. I compounded my trouble by covering it up with a lie. If I'd simply told the truth, I wouldn't have needed to fess up to messing up even more.

The choice is mine. I can either make things right and enjoy *clean plate living* or I can choose the slime of secrets, shame and guilt which escorted me into an eating disorder. Making things right keeps me healthy and happy. If I don't let slime in, it can't take over my life.

Lastly, I learned it's beyond mortifying to go back and make things right. Telling Dr. Freeman I'd lied was one of the hardest things I've ever done—and a great behavior modifier.

> *Going back and making things right is so mortifying you'll think twice before making it necessary to do so again.*

Pick

What about you? Do your actions line up with your values? Are you carrying around the guilt, shame and secrets of past wrongs?

Do you want to live without internal strife? Do you long for freedom, peace and joy? Do you want your energy freed to create a life you love?

The following tips will help you bounce back after you mess up as well as enable you to overcome negative emotions that hold you back from living fully in the present:

1. **Keep a clean plate.** Emotional clutter, like physical clutter, accumulates. Just as you need to take out the trash on a regular basis if you don't want rubbish overflowing onto the floor, you need to regularly clear out emotional garbage in order to prevent it from overtaking your life.

When you mess up but don't fess up, you dirty your plate. When you should do something but don't, you dirty your plate. When you go silent when someone hurts or angers you, you dirty your plate.

> *The bigger the problem, the bigger the pile of crud you add to your plate.*

Allow mess ups, disappointments and anger to pile up, and your plate is going to fill up. Sadly, each spoonful of accumulated crud leaves less and less room for good things to enter your life. Fill your plate to overflowing and your life, relationships and dreams quickly become mired in the muck.

Steps 8, 9 and 10 of Alcoholics Anonymous provide excellent guidelines for *clean plate living*.

Step 8: Make a list of all persons you've wronged and become willing to make amends to them all.

Step 9: Make direct amends whenever possible except for when to do so would injure them or someone else.

Step 10: Continue to take personal inventory and when you are wrong, promptly admit it.

Having worked the 12 Steps, I know firsthand the cost and courage of honesty and restitution. The only thing more expensive is choosing to live with the slime that accompanies bad behavior. It weighs you down and will prevent you from living life to the fullest.

All it took for me to be committed to *clean plate living* was one taste of the priceless peace and freedom it provided.

Steps 8, 9 and 10 loosened shame and guilt's stifling grips and allowed them to slide silently away from my soul. The price is far too high, and the freedom far too sweet for me to even entertain going backwards.

2. Deal with pain and anger directly and quickly. Just as secrets, shame and guilt hold you back, carrying around unresolved pain and anger will prevent you from creating the life you desire and deserve.

Contrary to popular belief, pain and anger aren't bad emotions. They are simply internal barometers that shout that something is wrong and needs to be addressed. You only get into trouble when you ignore them, when you inflict them on others, and when you allow them to build up and fester.

Pick

Any time you've retaliated in anger or spent more than 15 minutes hashing and rehashing what did or didn't happen, gather your courage and take action.

> *Time spent rehashing old wounds*
> *is stolen from time you could use*
> *accomplishing your dreams.*

3. **When someone hurts, angers or takes advantage of you:**

♦ **Nip it in the bud.** Deal with problems immediately and graciously. It's easiest to remain calm and courteous the first time something happens. If you let infractions build up, you're eventually going to blow up. Either that or you'll silently slither away, adding the heartache of a broken relationship to your life.

♦ **Use as normal a voice tone as possible when addressing concerns.** Avoid yelling, name calling and any other aggressive behavior.

♦ **Use "I" statements to address problems and ask for specific behavioral changes.** Kindly, but firmly let others know how their actions affect you and ask for the behavior you'd prefer.

The easiest way to learn "I" statements is to use *"A Bug and A Wish,"* a kid's template for expressing concerns and asking for a different behavior.

"A Bug and A Wish"
It bugs me when _____.
I wish you would _____.

For example:

It bugs me when you cut in line.
I wish you'd wait your turn.

It bugs me when you don't follow through.
I wish you'd do what you say.

It bugs me when you exclude me.
I wish you would include me.

As an adult with far more sophisticated thinking and language skills, you'll want to use "I" statements, the grown-up version of _"A Bug and A Wish."_

While following the same pattern, "I" statements allow for a wide range of feelings. They also recognize that not every requested behavior change is a wish, allowing for the times you want and need to make a stronger request.

"I" Statements
It _insert feeling word_ **me**
When you _insert troublesome behavior._
I need/would like/prefer _insert desired behavior._

91

Pick

Using the same examples from *"A Bug and A Wish"* illustrates the variations:

It *angers* me when *you cut in line*.
I'd *prefer you wait your turn*.

It *frustrates* me when *you don't follow through*.
I *need for you to do what you say*.

It *hurts* me when *you exclude me*.
I'd *like to be included*.

Here are a few more examples:

It *frightens* me when *you don't check in*.
I *need you to call when you're going to be late*.

It *hurts* me when *you take jabs at me*.
I'd *prefer you tell me directly when I've upset you*.

It *angers* me when *you snap at me*.
I *need you to tell me directly when you have a need*.

It *frustrates* me when *you lie*.
I *need you to tell the truth*.

"I" statements are significantly more effective and respectful than: "You're a complete jerk. I can't believe you said that to me in front of our friends. What were you thinking? How could you be so rude? Blah, blah, blah, blah, blah…"

The first time I used an "I" statement it took me two weeks to get up the courage to tell a roommate, "It frustrates me when you leave your dishes in the sink. I'd prefer you put them in the dishwasher."

While I've gotten much better over the years, there are still times it takes me awhile to get up my courage to address a problem, but the quicker I address things, the quicker I'm able to free up my energy to move forward, live life to the fullest and pursue my dreams.

Finding your voice and becoming a gentle truth teller can be frightening and feel very unnatural. Like any other behavior, the more you practice, the easier it becomes.

> *Have conversations as quickly and calmly as possible. Your dreams and best life are waiting for you.*

4. Master the art of "soft pillowing." When I told my roommate that the dishes in the sink frustrated me and that I'd prefer she put them in the dishwasher, icy silence ensued.

"Do you have a response?" I finally asked.

"I think it's pretty damn nitpicky," she angrily replied.

"You might be right," I answered, "***and*** I'd still prefer you put them in the dishwasher."

"Soft pillow" by absorbing what someone says, then gently push back by restating your original request. For example:

If someone tells you they think you're being un-reasonable, acknowledge they may be right ***and*** you still prefer the behavior change. If someone tells you that you

Pick

shouldn't feel the way you do, acknowledge they may be right *and* you still prefer the desired behavior change.

"**At the same time**" is also a wonderful phrase that acknowledges both individuals are important. For example:

"I understand you're busy, **at the same time**, I still need this done by the end of the day."

"I understand you want to spend money, **at the same time**, I need for us to stay within our budget."

"I understand you're angry, **at the same time**, I prefer we have a civil conversation."

5. **Expect resistance when you address concerns.** In an ideal world, once you've told another person how a specific behavior affects you, they apologize and make things right. By the same token, when you've hurt or angered someone and they care enough to risk your wrath or tears, you'll apologize and make things right.

Unfortunately, you don't live in an ideal world and many individuals will not be receptive to being held gently accountable for how their choices and actions impact you.

While it's still important you initiate the conversation, expect others to blow you off, get silent, pouty, angry or even abusive when you have the audacity to address a problem. When someone engages in bad behavior, use a second "I" statement to address their inappropriate response.

6. **"I" statements and "soft pillowing" work best with healthy individuals.** I've practiced "I" statements for almost 25 years. Even when people haven't liked hearing my concerns, the overwhelming majority have been respectful

and worked with me to create solutions that left both of us feeling valued and respected.

Sadly, not everyone is healthy or committed to creating win-win solutions when problems arise. There are people willing to win at all costs, bullies and abusers.

It took me almost 15 years of beating my head against a brick wall with a verbally abusive colleague to realize that "I" statements aren't always an effective, helpful or even viable strategy.

If a colleague becomes verbally aggressive calmly say, "The tone of this conversation is no longer professional."

If that doesn't work, tell them or anyone else who's being verbally aggressive you'll be happy to talk with them once they can converse civilly. If they are able to calm down and discuss things, great. If not, walk away until you're both able to address your differences respectfully.

If that doesn't work, pull in a powerful third party such as your boss, your boss' boss, a member of the clergy or a counselor.

> *It's amazing how much calmer a person can be when they don't want to look bad in front of someone else.*

If bringing in an objective third party doesn't enable you to settle the matter, set and hold appropriate boundaries. You may decide to only address problems with them in a public area, or to limit the topics you're willing to discuss. You may also choose to restrict or eliminate their access to you.

Pick

Silence may also be your best option after you've tried to address a concern as it can shame a verbally aggressive individual into seeing how badly they behave.

The only time I ever got an apology from my aggressive coworker was when I went silent in the middle of an attack. She came back the next week and apologized. I was so shocked you could have knocked me over with a feather. If I had figured out that strategy years earlier, that relationship would have been a lot less painful.

7. **Seek help immediately if you're on the receiving end of physical or verbal abusive.** Abuse is never acceptable, nor are you ever deserving of it. If you are in an abusive relationship, do what you must to stay safe and seek help from a trained professional immediately. It is extremely dangerous and almost impossible to engage in conflict resolution with an abusive person without ongoing professional support.

8. **Don't beat your head against a brick wall.** I firmly believe if two people care about each other and are willing to have tough, civil conversations, any problem can be resolved.

> *Relationships are either moving closer or farther apart. They don't stand still for long.*

You can't, however, force someone to work through a problem with you. If someone refuses to work through things with you, tell yourself the truth about where they are and what they are and aren't ready, willing or able to do.

Mourn the loss that such a refusal entails, and stop repeatedly reopening yourself to perpetual pain.

Protect yourself emotionally by setting appropriate boundaries. Creating some distance will help you to get off the rollercoaster ride, and prevent you from participating in the battering of your heart and self-esteem. Distance also enables you to keep communication channels open which can eventually lead to full reconciliation.

Life is too short and your dreams are far too precious to squander your time and energy carrying around guilt, shame, regret, anger, resentment or bitterness. While you can't control what happens to you, you alone are responsible for how you respond and for managing your emotions.

Pick to fess up when you mess up.

Pick to have tough conversations.

Pick to live guilt free.

Chapter 9

Frozen or Free:
Forgive

"Forgiveness is a gift we give ourselves,
setting us free to live fully in the present."
Sherene McHenry

My heart was broken. I'd fallen in love with a handsome, charming man who, despite blatantly flirting with me, was only interested in being my friend. I was embarrassed. I was hurt. I was angry. I just couldn't figure out if I was angrier with myself or with him.

"How could you be so stupid?" I chastised myself.

"You should have known he wouldn't love you," my internal *mean girl* taunted.

Hurt and confused, I tried to talk to him. He disappeared. I fumed.

"How dare he play with my heart?"

Pick

Wanting to be free to move forward, I tried not thinking about him. I tried keeping busy. I tried letting go. I tried forgiving him. Nothing worked. I couldn't find a way out of my anger.

Left festering, my anger became bitterness. Its bile slowly seeped into my soul, mixing with my longing for him to wake up and see how great I was.

I began to notice I was changing. My tolerance for frustration tanked. Resentment choked my joy. I was becoming an angry woman. Someone I'd never been. Someone I didn't like.

One day, I sat in my living room crying out to God. "I don't like who I'm becoming. I've lost my joy. I'm hurt and angry all the time. I don't know how to forgive him. I don't know how to be free. Help me, God."

As I sat staring at the golden light ushered in by the evening sun, I got my answer. *Terminate him.* Sounded good to me.

I opened my computer and immediately typed a letter saying everything I needed to say. By the time I finished and hit send, the bitterness was gone. I was free.

I learned a great deal from my walk through my anger and bitterness. Specifically, if I want to create a life I love, I can't afford to get stuck behind bitterness, anger, resentment or regret.

Festering, unresolved negative emotions drown dreams and diminish joy. The daily challenges of life, relationships, and pursuing hopes are hard enough to navigate without lugging around the weight of unforgiveness.

I found that I can refuse to forgive or I can choose to let go of past pains. The choice is mine. No one can make another person forgive. If I choose to forgive, I reap the benefits. If I choose to live with bitterness and anger, I pay the price.

In addition, I need to forgive myself. Beating myself up does nothing to make me feel better or to change the situation. It just squanders my emotional resources. I need to accept my imperfections and tendency to mess up. Choosing to forgive myself frees me from the past and sets me up for future success.

I also need to forgive others. Otherwise, I tie my life to theirs as well as to the past. Choosing to forgive frees me to focus on the future and provides a path to peace and happiness. When I choose not to forgive I forgo the very things that make life sweeter.

What about you? Are you angry, hurt or depressed? Are you resentful and bitter? Do you have a hard time forgiving others for what they've done to you and to those you love? Do you struggle to forgive yourself?

Do you wonder what forgiveness even looks like? Do you fear if you forgive someone you give them a free pass? Do you cling to your hurts in order to inflict pain on the other person? Do you long to be free?

Whether you're good at forgiving yourself and others or if the very thought of forgiveness feels like failure, the following will help you better understand forgiveness and set you up for future success:

Pick

1. **Choose to forgive others.** When you refuse to forgive others, you tie your life to the past like an anchor tethered to a boat. You'll never be fully free to create a life you love if you refuse to let go.

Confusion exists over what forgiving someone does and doesn't mean. Forgiving doesn't mean forgetting; it simply means letting go of resentment and forgoing your desire for revenge.

Forgiving doesn't necessarily mean reconciliation either. Forgiveness is something you can do on your own whereas reconciliation takes two parties. Lastly, forgiveness isn't necessarily a feeling. Forgiveness is a conscious decision you make and sometimes have to remake and remake each time a painful memory rears its ugly head.

If you haven't already done so, share your concerns with the offender and see if they are willing to work with you to make things right. If they are—great. Problem resolved. Relationship restored.

If they aren't ready, willing or able, free yourself emotionally by choosing to forgive them—not for their benefit, but for your own. If you want to create a life you love, you can't afford to squander your time and energy dragging around resentment, revenge or hatred.

> *If you don't extend forgiveness to others, it rarely returns to you.*

Forgiving someone who has hurt or angered you can be a lot easier said than done. When I'm faced with needing to forgive someone, I find it helpful to remember that when I mess up I want others to forgive me. That's usually all it takes for me to make the decision to forgive and let things go.

When remembering that I want to be forgiven doesn't do the trick, I pray for help to forgive the person who has wronged me. My prayer is, "God, I'm mad and hurt for a good reason. While I can't forgive them on my own, I'm willing to be willing to forgive."

There have only been a few times when my heart hasn't changed within three days of praying for the willingness to forgive. When I find that I'm still incapable of forgiving someone, I *terminate or reposition* them by saying what I need to say in a letter that I may never choose to send.

I've written a handful of termination/repositioning letters over the past decade and I've only sent a few of them. Sent or not, upon the completion of each letter I was immediately released from the resentment, pain and bitterness I had been carrying, sometimes for years.

Termination/Repositioning Letter Format

♦ **What I liked about you.** There are reasons you let this person into your life. Take time to remember and write down all the things you like/liked about them. For example, "I love how carefree you are and that you never let things get you down. I also appreciate how much fun we had together. You always made me laugh…"

♦ **What I've learned from you.** Write out all you've learned from them—the good, the bad and the ugly. "From you I've learned how healing honesty can be.

I've also learned how painful it is when someone disappears without an explanation…"

♦ **What I need for you to know.** Here's where you get to express what you need to say as honestly and as gently as you can. For example, "I wish you could understand that your silence is far more painful than anything you could have said. I also wish you could have understood how much I cared for you and our relationship…"

♦ **What I hope for you.** In this portion, tell them your wishes for them and for the relationship. For example, "My hope is that you will one day learn to have tough conversations without disappearing. I also hope that you will experience rich, honest and rewarding relationships…"

♦ **Thank you and goodbye.** Thank them for the part they've played in your life and growth, and then end your letter. For example, "Thank you for the part you played in my life. I have grown in wisdom and character because of you."

You'll know your termination letter is done when you've said everything you needed to say without any jabs or wounding sarcasm. Write and rewrite your letter until all statements intended to hurt or shame the other person are gone. Then determine if you want to send it. It's up to you. The letter is for your benefit and freedom.

While such a letter may seem simplistic, the results are instantaneous.

A termination letter accomplishes multiple goals. It allows you to say what you need to say fully, without interruption. That alone can be extremely healing. It also enables you to remember the relationship from beginning to end which counters the natural tendency to focus only on the negative parts of a relationship once it goes bad.

Perhaps the greatest benefit of a termination letter is that it moves you from being a victim to being empowered and wiser. While such wisdom comes at an extremely high price, it is invaluable and sets you up for future success.

> *While forgiveness may never come easily,*
> *the more you practice doing it,*
> *the easier it becomes.*

2. Forgive yourself. It's just as important to forgive yourself as it is to forgive others if you want to create a life you love. Messing up is part of being human. You're going to do it at every job you ever have and in every relationship with any length or depth. Learn to be gentle with yourself.

> *Being gentle means forgiving yourself when you*
> *mess up. We should learn from our mistakes, but*
> *we shouldn't beat the tar out of ourselves over*
> *them. The past is just that, the past. Learn what*
> *went wrong and why. Make amends if you need*
> *to. Then drop it and move on.*
>
> *Sean Covey*

Pick

Messing up doesn't make you a bad person; it simply means you're human. It's when you refuse to forgive yourself that you tie your life to the past and prevent yourself from reaching your full potential. Cut yourself some slack on messing up, but never on fessing up and doing what it takes to make things right.

Ask yourself two questions when you get stuck and are having a hard time forgiving yourself:

♦ Did I do the best I could with the time, talent and resources I had available?

♦ If I had the chance to do it over, would I do it differently?

Being able to answer "yes" to either question allows you to accept that you are a fallible human being and sets you up for future success. Learning from your mistakes and choosing to not repeat them ensures that you are wiser and frees you to fully engage in creating a life you love.

Pick to forgive others.

Pick to forgive yourself.

Pick to be free.

Chapter 10

Hurtful or Helpful: Embrace Healthy Coping Strategies

"If you want satisfaction and success,
cut down self-inflicted stress."

Sherene McHenry

Couch potato. A fitting, albeit discouraging label. Dressed in baggy pajamas, I hunkered down with the remote in one hand and a big bowl of salty potato chips on the coffee table. Add a pillow, blanket and space heater to keep my toes toasty and I was ready for a marathon of mindless, mind numbing distraction.

I would turn on the TV when I woke up "just to check the weather." Yeah, right. Unless I had somewhere to go, hours later I'd find myself gazing at the screen with glassy eyes. In the evenings I'd plop down and almost before I knew it, the wee hours of morning arrived.

Over the years, potato chips and television became close companions easing my isolation, hiding my exhaustion, and deadening the disappointment of unfulfilled dreams.

Movie after movie, stupid show after stupid show, I became increasingly numb. Except for the guilt. No matter how many shows I watched, I knew I was made for more.

Life is too short to live in front of the television. That's what I wrote after Melinda's murder. Yet I sat in front of mine for hours on end. Wasting my time. Wasting my potential. Wasting my life.

"Just one more show, then I'll work on my book," I'd lie to myself time and time again.

"What's wrong with me?" I questioned. "Why can't I turn my dreams and longings into reality?"

"Because you burn your free time in front of the boob tube." I answered harshly.

"I know. Maybe tomorrow I'll do better."

"I certainly hope so. The clock's ticking. Years are sliding by."

"I'll try harder."

Repeated regularly, I added a little more discouragement and an ever harsher, critical, condemning tone with each ensuing day. My brain knew I needed to change. My body knew I needed to change. My heart knew I needed to change.

Change didn't come easily. As is generally the case, weaning myself away from my maladaptive coping mechanism of too much television and junk food has been a process of one step forward and two steps back.

Three things have helped me minimize and overcome my monsters: Working with a therapist, fully pursuing my dreams, and setting clear internal boundaries.

Here's what I've learned as I've traded in my unhealthy coping mechanisms for healthier ones that help get me closer to where I need and want to go.

I need to do what's within my power to prevent becoming overwhelmed, exhausted and discouraged. When I feel good, I don't need to zone out of life. It's that simple. Being nice to myself, letting go of perfectionism and taking care of my body all minimize my desire to zone out.

The battle is won or lost long *before* I turn on the television or open a bag of chips. Deciding not to bring chips into my house sets me up for success. So does having vegetables I can chomp on ready to go in my refrigerator.

I've also learned not to turn the television on until after 8:30 at night. If I can't stop myself, my backup plan is to get out of the house until the temptation passes.

Now that I'm not mindlessly syphoning off my time to television viewing, it's amazing how much better I feel and how much more I'm accomplishing. As an added bonus, after years of struggling, my dreams are finally coming to fruition.

> *The battle to overcome unhealthy coping mechanisms is won or lost before it begins. Set yourself up for success.*

Pick

What about you? Do you find yourself regularly engaging in zone-out activities? Are old habits keeping you from accomplishing your dreams and creating a life you love? Do you feel trapped?

Are people in your life expressing concerns about what you are and aren't doing? Do you repeatedly do things you know aren't good for you? Are your choices ruining your relationships, life or dreams?

Do you long to live life to the fullest? Do you want to be happy, healthy and energetic? Do you want to captain your ship instead of floating aimlessly at the whim and fancy of how you feel? If so, there are concrete things you can do to set yourself up for success and enable yourself to overcome crippling coping mechanisms:

1. **Tell yourself and someone else the truth about what you're doing and how often you're doing it.** Perhaps you're like me, jeopardizing your hopes and dreams watching too much television. Maybe you're experiencing an eating disorder. You could be a compulsive shopper.

Whether you're self-medicating with alcohol, sex, food, gambling, shopping, thrill seeking, workaholism or any other "ism," tell yourself the truth. Your behavior is getting in the way of your creating a life you love.

Most importantly, listen to those closest to you. If they're expressing concern about you or indicating your actions are adversely affecting them—again—tell yourself the truth. You have a problem and it's time to do something different.

2. Identify and resolve underlying issues. Work with a physician to determine if health problems are a concern. If they are, address them head on. Getting my thyroid and adrenals working properly and taking vitamin B significantly improved my energy levels and helped get me off the couch.

In the same vein, unpack emotional baggage that's weighing you down. Resolve relationship problems. Release destructive emotions. Reverse negative situations.

If you can't overcome what's holding you back on your own, invest in a tune up or engage in significant work with a counselor or life coach. Your dreams and those you love deserve the best of you, not a self-medicated version.

> *Life is too short and the stakes are too high to navigate it numbly.*

3. Minimize self-inflicted stress. Live proactively by focusing on things you can control, setting appropriate boundaries with yourself and others, developing healthier relationships, and reducing your emotional and physical clutter. The healthier you are, the less you'll need to self-medicate.

4. Combat life stressors with healthy coping strategies. Unhealthy coping strategies delay and derail dreams and life satisfaction. Healthy strategies position you to create and enjoy a life you love. The following are suggestions that will help you manage what life throws your way.

Pick

♦ **Get adequate sleep, exercise regularly and eat healthy foods.** Adequate energy is essential if you're going to create a life you love. Relationships take energy, chasing your dreams takes energy, daily functioning takes energy.

If you want to maximize your energy, treat your body well. It is well known that exercising regularly, eating healthy foods and getting adequate rest helps you feel better, enhances your thinking and increases your level of energy.

♦ **Keep a journal.** Studies show that writing about negative emotions decreases them. The next time you are hurt or angry, instead of stewing, write out your thoughts and the things you'd like to say. While you may be emotionally exhausted afterwards, you won't have nearly as many negative thoughts and emotions running through you.

To get maximum benefit out of journaling, you must be able to write freely. Privacy is paramount. If you're afraid of hurting others, shred, burn or bury the pages when you are finished writing. Or, make a pact with a trusted friend to destroy your journals upon your death. You'll know what you need to do.

All you need to get started is something to write with or a computer. I personally prefer using a spiral bound journal that opens flat.

+ **Be still.** You're going to encounter numerous problems on your way to success. Uninterrupted periods of stillness empower your brain to create solutions. Additionally, dreams take time to formulate. It's amazing what your brain will bubble up in silence.

Create pockets of stillness by turning off your TV, smart phone and computer. Regardless of how it feels, the world won't come to an end. If others can reach you any time of the day and night, they will.

> *Technology is a wonderful tool,*
> *but it makes a terrible master.*

I challenge you to unplug for at least an hour a day. You'll grow to enjoy your own company and hearing your thoughts. You'll also be less stressed and more fun to be around.

+ **Slow down.** In our fast food, rapidly paced society, there's a great deal of pressure to go, go, go, faster, faster, faster. If you run like a hamster on a wheel, rest assured that down time is critical for creating a life you love.

> *One of the great illusions of our day is*
> *that hurrying will buy us more time.*
> *John Ortberg*

+ **Prioritize.** Focus on what's truly important. Not everything needs to be done today, nor does everything need to be done flawlessly. If it's brain

113

surgery, you better get it right. At the same time, a 93% in school earns you the same A as a 100%.

As you differentiate between what does and doesn't demand perfection, you'll be happier and easier to be around.

♦ **Use your vacation days.** Many forgo vacation because they have too much to do or they don't think it's safe to take time away from their job. Only you know the climate at your work place, but you do need time away from work, even if it's just a day at home.

> *Recharging your batteries regularly increases your life satisfaction, sense of well- being, energy, creativity, and productivity.*

A good friend of mine is married to a successful, high level executive who works extremely long hours. Even though he's great at playing on the weekends, he gets grumpy when he works day after day, week after week, month after month, without a break.

Being proactive, they recently began scheduling one long weekend a month for mini vacations. They've also blocked out when he'll take his vacation for the next year. He's happier and more productive and she's happier too.

♦ **Take a day of rest.** Make a habit of taking one day a week off from work. You'll increase your energy and creativity, decrease your stress and your family and friends will be thrilled as you take time for them. I take Sundays off and am amazed at how much more motivated and productive I am on Mondays.

Set-backs, stress, disappointments, pain and anger are all part of life. If you want to create a life you love, deal with them wisely. Unhealthy coping habits hold you back. Productive strategies propel you forward. The choice is yours. The stakes are high.

Pick to cope carefully.

Pick to be proactive.

Pick to be highly productive.

Chapter 11

Apathetic or Energetic: Get Happy

"Don't waste your life waiting to be happy."
Sherene McHenry

I am not a morning person. I've never been a morning person. I'm not sure I want to be a morning person. Since childhood, my morning mantra has been "just five more minutes." I still savor hitting snooze and relish the gentleness of waking up slowly. Hunkering down in a toasty bed makes me happy.

Once I've lingered as long as I dare, I get out of bed, shuffle to the kitchen and start a pot of coffee. As the minutes pass and the caffeine kicks in, I begin to perk up. My mind works faster. My smile comes quicker. My sense of humor returns.

Despite my lifelong desire for leisurely mornings, I followed my father's advice in college, "Start your classes at

Pick

8:00 a.m., Sherene. You'll be done by noon and the rest of the day will be yours."

While it wasn't easy, I did it. Every semester. That is until my senior year. Having knocked out most of my required courses, I finally had the luxury of scheduling my classes to begin midmorning. It was going to be a great year.

Several weeks into my relaxed morning routine, our cheerleading coach announced mandatory, 6:30 a.m. aerobic sessions. I cried. I got angry. I begged. I dragged my feet. Nothing changed. If I wanted to cheer, I'd be exercising at the crack of dawn.

Immensely frustrated about the disruption to my carefully planned schedule, not to mention the hours the workouts would add to my already busy life, I didn't even bother to say hello the first morning. I was unhappy and I didn't care who knew it.

After three gut-wrenching days, I came to a realization. I could be miserable or I could be happy. The choice was mine. The only common denominator was that I would be exercising at 6:30 a.m. I picked happy.

Once I decided to have fun, things changed dramatically for me. I laughed. I joked. I grew closer to my squad. Filled with friends, the mornings became enjoyable. Looking back, I remember those 6:30 a.m. exercise sessions fondly.

I learned several lessons by being forced to do something I would never have chosen. Lessons I continue to employ to this very day. First, while I don't always get a say in what happens to or around me, I always get to pick my attitude. I can make the best of things, or I can be miserable and make things harder.

I'm not perfect and I still struggle with initial resistance to imposed events and circumstances. However, once I tell myself the truth about how things are going to be, the vast majority of the time I choose to make what I'm doing fun.

As a professor, the first night of every class I'd say, "My expectation is that we'll work hard, and that we'll have a lot of fun in the process. The only given is that we're going to be here every week. It's up to us if we decide to enjoy it." The overwhelming majority of my students chose fun and I loved laughing with them.

I also learned that happiness is a choice. In any situation, I can choose to be miserable, or I can choose to be happy.

With the imposed exercise program, I could have chosen to be angry all year, grumbled every morning and made sure everyone around me was equally miserable. But I'm the one who would have suffered most and lost my joy in the process. I get one ride on this planet. That's all. I pick to be happy.

> *Happiness is a conscious choice, not*
> *an automatic response.*
> *Mildred Barthel*

What about you? Are you angry? Chronically unhappy? Do you take your misery out on others? What would your family, friends and coworkers say about you?

Pick

Or, are you happy? Do you have infectious energy? Do people like to be around you? Are you able to make lemonade out of lemons?

The following are tips to help you choose to make the best of any situation and have more fun in all aspects of your life:

1. **Recognize your happiness isn't based on what you own, your job or any external condition.** While winning the lottery, losing 10 pounds or getting a new toy, relationship or job may make you happy for a brief time, happiness based on external circumstances never lasts.

The thrill of new possessions wears off, people let you down and jobs can become mundane. Basing your happiness on external things leaves you at the whim and fancy of others, circumstances and what you own. You are far too powerful to put yourself in such a powerless position.

> *Happiness based on external circumstances is always fleeting.*

2. **Focus on things that truly matter.** While things are certainly nice to have and losing weight is great, they aren't what truly matters in the end.

I've yet to hear of anyone dying who said, "Wow, I sure am glad I got that nice, new car" or "Losing those 10 pounds totally transformed my life." As life comes to a close, people focus on the quality of their relationships and whether or not they lived a life that mattered.

Develop reciprocal relationships and surround yourself with healthy individuals, you'll naturally be happier. And, the happier you are, the more attractive you'll be to healthy individuals.

Live a life that aligns with your values, beliefs and talents, and you'll be happier. Focus on things that have lasting value and you'll be happier. The choice is yours. Pick.

3. Learn to be content with what you have. If you want to be happy, learn to be content with what you have. Being content is about focus. If you focus on what others have or what your life lacks, you will never be happy. Focus on all the things you have and the blessings that abound in your life, and you will find happiness.

A dear friend recently built a beautiful home. After touring it, I left wondering how some people could have so much while others have so little. I hate to admit it, but I wasn't thinking about orphans, the homeless or the truly impoverished. I was thinking about myself. What a laugh.

When I find myself comparing what I have to others or wanting more, I remind myself that I am exceptionally blessed and extremely wealthy by world standards. So are you if you had plenty to eat today and shelter to sleep in.

It's foolish and unproductive to waste your life waiting to be happy until you achieve or acquire something.

4. Develop an attitude of gratitude. Closely related to being content with what you have is developing an attitude of gratitude. Begin to create an attitude of gratitude by noticing the things that are good, helpful and right in your life.

Pick

Take time daily to acknowledge at least three things for which you are grateful. On tough days, your gratitude list might be as basic as food, shelter and oxygen.

I'm far happier when I list and take time to thank God for all the wonderful things He has provided. While I don't do it nearly enough, when I pick to express my gratitude verbally, I have far more energy and enjoy an increased sense of well-being that carries throughout the day.

5. **Live well.** While it takes hard work, living well frees you to create a life you love which naturally increases your happiness.

Living well includes such things as getting real, finding your voice, surrounding yourself with supportive individuals, setting boundaries, living your dreams and values, fessing up when you mess up and learning to say no. Living well also includes taking care of yourself, being kind and helping others.

A good friend once lamented how much work it takes to live well. He's right. I've yet to meet someone who has created a life they love without a lot of hard work.

"Is it really worth it?" he questioned.

"Absolutely," I replied. "Living well is like climbing a lighthouse. It takes a lot of effort to go around and around, especially in the beginning when it doesn't look like you're making much progress. The good news is, as the circles get smaller, the view—like life—gets better and better."

6. **Engage in activities that give you joy.** If you want to be cheerful and energetic, regularly engage in activities that make you happy. Just as you need to fill your car's gas tank if

you want to keep driving, you need to fill your fun tank if you want to be happy and energetic.

Identify three things you love to do. Things that make you smile with the sheer joy of living. Three activities that remind you that even though life can be hard, it's great to be alive. I personally love the sun on my face and the wind in my hair. Skiing, boating and being out in nature never fail to fill me with joy and contentment.

What about you? Have you identified three activities that make you happy? Great. Now comes the test. When was the last time you engaged in one of your favorite activities?

When I ask audiences this question, I hear a collective gasp. It's easy to forget to take time to feed your soul through play when life is hectic or you're focused on work, chasing a dream, parenting or paying the bills.

> *Fostering your spirit of play will help*
> *you make it through the day.*

Choosing to regularly engage in activities that give you joy requires you to know yourself, to value yourself and to budget your time and resources accordingly.

Make play an ongoing part of your life by doing a minimum of one fun activity a month. Even better, find a way to incorporate at least one fun activity into every week or even every day. As long as you don't go overboard, blow your budget or start under-functioning, your life satisfaction and energy levels will greatly increase.

Pick

> *Fun is a daily vitamin*
> *no one should miss.*

7. Schedule time for yourself. If you're a planner and wired with a strong sense of responsibility, it is imperative that you schedule fun and have something on your calendar you're looking forward to doing.

I once worked with a discouraged client suffering from low levels of depression. Like many women, it frustrated her that she gave and gave to others, but never had time for the things she wanted to do. Knowing she was a planner, I suggested she schedule time for herself on her calendar at the beginning of each week. She agreed.

The following week she was beaming. She even giggled as she described the luxury of taking a bubble bath and reading a book.

If you're serious by nature and tempted to pass on play, consider the following benefits before you short change yourself any longer.

◆ **You'll increase your creativity and productivity.** Your brain needs down time. When you give it a break and combine that break with the rush that comes from having fun, you'll get far more done than if you keep plodding along.

◆ **You'll improve your energy level.** Closely related to increased creativity and productivity, you will have more energy which will allow you to work even harder.

♦ **You'll experience a heightened sense of well-being.** In this uncertain, topsy-turvy world, it is extremely important to be reminded that life is more than work and chores. Play reminds me that no matter how stressful my day is or how terrible the nightly news, life is worth living.

♦ **You'll strengthen your relationships.** In addition to being a happier more energetic you, when you find fun activities that you can do as a couple, as a family and with friends you strengthen your relationships. You'll be surprised at the powerful glue shared play provides.

> *The family that plays together tends to stay together.*

Unless you are intentional, the very act of living will diminish your happiness and the energy you have to devote to the things that matter most. Today's world is scary, careers and relationships take work and bad things happen.

Regardless of what's taking place around you or what's happening to you, you alone pick your attitude. Regularly feeding your spirit of play makes it easier to make attitude adjustments. You also get to choose whether you're going to be content with what you have or if you're going to squander your life chasing illusions.

Pick to be content.

Pick to foster your spirit of play.

Pick to have fun and be happy.

Chapter 12

Hassle or Humor: Learn to Laugh

"I realize humor isn't for everyone. It's only for people who want to have fun, enjoy life, and feel alive."
Anne Wilson Schaef

W hile I've met some very nice men, I've also met a few doozies in the dating pool. The following is a list of things men have said to me, most within two minutes of our having met:

"I quit drinking two weeks ago." Lucky me.

"I lost my license." Does that mean I get to drive?

"All the men in my family died in their 40's." We're almost 50.

"I declared bankruptcy this week." That's sexy.

"You're the answer to my prayers about my finances." What about my prayers?

"My ex is psycho." How promising.

Pick

"My kids are a mess." That should be fun.

"I don't have a job." I get to take care of you?

"My ex gave me an incurable STD." Oh my, look at the time.

Shocking they were all still single, isn't it?

When it comes to dating and many other things in life, I can either laugh, cry or tear out my hair. Finding laughter in trying or frustrating circumstances not only makes things more fun, it can also diminish disappointment and enable me to press forward when I'm tempted to throw in the towel.

Laughter also helps me roll with the punches and lessens my anxieties. I want to find Mr. Right. I really do. In order to do that, I know I need to stay open and happy. Humor helps. A lot.

I fell in love with making others laugh long ago. When I keep my eyes open, every day experiences provide great fodder. When I'm able to laugh at myself and the things that happen to me, others generally join in.

What about you? Are you in the midst of trying circumstances? Do you wish you were happier? Have you lost your funny bone somewhere along life's journey?

Do you long to laugh? Has it been so long since you've laughed that you've forgotten how fun laughter can be?

Do you want to be healthier and happier? Do you want to be better equipped to cope with life's stressors? Do you want to improve your relationships? Do you want to be free to move forward?

Hassle or Humor

Research reveals that humor is incredibly powerful. It's been shown to increase circulation, aid immune systems and reduce pain. In addition, humor releases tension, eases worries, provides hope, aids in coping and improves quality of life. If all that weren't enough, humor also unites us, improves relationships and allows us to move forward.

The following are ways you can strategically add humor to your life and reap its benefits:

1. **Seek and find humor.** If you're not laughing at yourself and things happening around you on a regular basis, you're missing out. Pay attention to what you and others are saying, as well as doing and you'll discover plays on words, double meanings and opportunities for delightful one-liners.

2. **Embrace your quirkiness.** Admit it, you're quirky. Everyone is quirky. Once you determine you're delightfully quirky, you free yourself to laugh at all the silly things you do.

3. **Tell on yourself and allow others to laugh with you.** My sister is the master of letting others laugh with her. She'll call me and say, "You'll never believe what I just did..." She makes me laugh so hard I snort.

People want to be around people who are charmingly human and able to laugh at themselves.

4. **Watch or read something funny.** My sister's favorite movie is *Elf.* We watch it with her every year just to share her joy. She laughs so hard she can barely breathe which makes it all the funnier for the rest of us. My brother and

Pick

brother-in-law on the other hand love *Dumb and Dumber*. They crack each other up trading lines and talking about scenes.

You know what tickles your funny bone, tickle it on a regular basis.

> *Find someone who'll laugh with you and you'll chuckle even more.*

5. **Scan the funny pages.** It's amazing how the best cartoonists can make us laugh in seconds. Clip comics that amuse you and when you need a quick laugh you can enjoy them again and again.

6. **Make funny faces in the mirror.** Embrace your inner child and see how long it takes you to make yourself laugh. Who needs a comic when you can get a jump start on a great day by simply clowning around?

If you want to live on the wild side and get outrageous, Steve Rizzo suggests standing naked in front of the mirror and proclaiming, "I'm ready for the day." Just don't terrorize any children or small animals in the process.

7. **Tell jokes and funny stories.** Good jokes and well told stories can make people laugh so hard their sides split. Even pitiful puns, as long as they aren't too plentiful, bring smiles and chuckles.

> *Practice your material and weed out the unimportant details. The tighter the joke or story, the funnier.*

I limit my joke telling as I inevitably butcher punch lines. If you jumble up a joke, laugh at yourself and let others join in. If you don't do it too often, your mess up may be even funnier than your joke.

8. Smile. Grinning like a fool, even if there's nothing funny, will almost instantly improve your mood. Try it now, for 10 seconds if you don't believe me.

Smile at your desk. Smile while you're doing chores. Smile when you're stuck in traffic. Smile for no reason other than to smile. You'll be happier and everyone else will wonder what you're up to.

> *The more the corners of your lips turn up, the happier you'll feel.*

9. Choose laughter. Bad and stressful things happen in everyone's life. When you're in the midst of a trying time, you always get a choice. You can give in to pain, frustration or fear, or you can choose to find the laughter.

10. Avoid inappropriate humor. While the benefits of humor are many, there are times when humor is inappropriate. For example, it's never okay to use humor or sarcasm to wound others. If you're angry or hurt, talk to the person rather than blindside them under the guise of a joke.

By the same token, if you find yourself on the receiving end of hurtful humor, initiate a civil "chat". As stated previously, bad behavior left unchecked grows. Hold yourself and others accountable when humor is used as a weapon.

Pick

Lastly, while I'm sure you're aware that racial and ethnic jokes are never acceptable, there are several groups that are still regularly the target of wounding humor. The next time you're tempted to "male bash," tell a joke about someone who's overweight, blond or religious, ask yourself if it's okay to tell the same joke about a racial group. If the answer is no, don't tell it.

You might be thinking, "Lighten up, Sherene, it's just a joke." To you perhaps, but not to the group negatively affected by such jokes. If you're thinking, "But it's true, men (blonds, Republicans, Democrats...) are xyz." Yes, and so are some women, brunettes and members of every ethnicity, religion and political party.

It boils down to treating others the way you want to be treated. You'll never go wrong with respect and kindness.

When someone blushes with embarrassment.
When someone carries away an ache.
When something sacred is made to appear common.
When someone's weakness provides the laughter.
When profanity is required to make it funny.
When a child is brought to tears.
When everyone can't join in the laughter.
It's a poor joke.
Cliff Thomas

Hassle or Humor

Regularly incorporate humor into your life and your productivity and resiliency will grow by leaps and bounds. You'll move yourself closer to creating a life you love.

Pick to find humor in life's circumstances.

Pick to be respectful.

Pick to laugh.

Chapter 13

Craving or Contentment: Cultivate Spirituality

"No one in the world can alter truth.
All we can do is seek it and live it."
                                    St. Maximilian Kolbe

For as far back as I can remember, I felt guilty. As a young child I did things I knew were wrong including stealing cookies, lashing out in anger and lying. Fearful of hell, I invited Jesus into my life around age seven. While I recall feeling relieved, my fears and guilt remained intact.

As I grew, I continued to do things I knew were wrong. I'd pray for forgiveness, but I knew deep inside I was a bad person and that the things I'd done were too big to be forgiven.

Years passed, growing my guilt and shame. It got so bad that whenever I couldn't find someone, I experienced

Pick

rapture anxiety, the gut retching fear that Jesus had returned but left me behind.

I longed for peace, joy and freedom, but I couldn't find them anywhere. Not in a nice home, nor in a good job, my education or a great guy. While peace, joy and freedom eluded me, my anxiety, emptiness and guilt grew.

It wasn't until I began to work the 12 steps of Alcoholic Anonymous that I found what I had spent my entire life searching for: Peace, acceptance, forgiveness, freedom and joy.

I'll never forget *Step 4: Take a searching and fearless moral inventory of myself.* I filled page after page writing down everything I'd ever done wrong. Wanting complete freedom, I left nothing out.

Seeing my guilt in black and white was sobering and painful. It was even harder and more humbling to risk *Step 5: Admit to God, to ourselves and to another human being the exact nature of my wrongs*, by sharing my actions and failures with my sponsor, Alice.

I thought I'd be able to hand her my sheets of shame and that she would silently read them and grant me absolution. That wasn't the case.

"Read them," she requested.

"No," I declined.

"Read them," she repeated more forcefully.

"No," I refused again, head hung in shame.

"Read them," she commanded.

"Okay" I agreed huffily, needing her to back off.

I read my sin and shame to her in their totality. Leaving no humiliating detail out, I was embarrassed. I was humiliated. I was mortified.

To my amazement, after almost everything I shared, she said, "I did that." I wasn't alone. Nor was I the worst person on the planet. Hope began to emerge.

Step 6: Be entirely ready to have God remove all my defects of character, was an easy one for me. I'd carried my shame with me every day of my life. I was ready for freedom and forgiveness.

Kneeling together by her couch, I completed *Step 7: Humbly ask Him to remove my shortcomings.* For the first time in my life I was able to accept and feel God's forgiveness. Peace and joy flooded in where guilt and shame had long reigned. Hope ignited. I was free.

While I still mess up, hurt others and do shameful things, for almost a quarter of a century I've re-experienced forgiveness and freedom each time I confess my short-comings. Peace surrounds my soul. Joy bubbles forth. Freedom reigns.

Just between us, I have to tell you, while I don't fully understand God and why so many bad things happen in this world, I feel like I'm one of His favorite children. His love and delight in me give me great joy. Scandalous sounding, isn't it?

I once told someone how I felt and they looked at me in horror. Please hear me right. It's not because I'm special, it's because He loves each of us so very much. The problem is, so many of us hide from Him in our shame and confusion over who He is and what He does and doesn't do.

I'm profoundly grateful for the 12 Steps and my spiritual journey. They radically changed my life. It took me a long time to find peace, hope and joy. Life is hard and I don't know how I would have made it through without them.

Along the way I've learned religion can be distorted. For whatever reason, the primary message I heard was that I was bad and God was waiting to zap me for every misstep. Shame and guilt colored how I saw myself and bled into every aspect of my life.

My belief that I was the only person who struggled kept me isolated from God and others. Breaking the silence and learning that I wasn't alone radically changed my life. Letting go of shame and guilt freed me to fully accept forgiveness and grace. Until I shared my shame and guilt with a healthy, safe person, however, I stayed trapped.

What about you? Have you been left damaged and disillusioned by religion or religious people? Does even thinking about God make you angry or nervous?

Do you struggle with guilt, shame and remorse? Do you long to experience peace, hope and joy? Do you ever feel empty and restless? Do you struggle with being unsatisfied? Does your heart whisper, "There has to be more?"

If you are among the broken or isolated or feel "There has to be more," I encourage you to cultivate your spirituality.

A dear friend who enjoys all the trappings of success including living her dreams, having a great husband, happy and successful adult children, a beautiful home, nice vacations and expensive cars started her spiritual journey because "Something was missing".

Spirituality is an aspect of life that is easy to ignore, especially when things are going well.

If you're like many, you're thinking, "No way am I exploring spirituality. I've seen far too many people hurt by organized religion." You're right, far too many have been injured and manipulated in the name of religion. The good news is that not all faith is toxic.

If you're one of the millions left damaged and disillusioned by people you trusted, by scandal, impropriety, rules, rigidity, judgment and only feeling you measure up if you're perfect, I urge you to:

1. Consider the benefits of embracing spiritual practices. Research reveals that regularly engaging in spiritual activities produces health benefits. Specifically, individuals who attend church weekly and pray daily have lower blood pressure, experience less physical pain and have stronger immune systems than their non-spiritual counterparts.

In addition, they are hospitalized less frequently, are less likely to suffer depression, and when they do become depressed, they are more likely to recover. Lastly, they enjoy a greater sense of well-being and live, on average, eight years longer than others.

Perhaps you're surprised by the benefits of regularly engaging in spiritual activities. You may also be wondering how spirituality can make such a daily difference. Explanations include that in addition to grounding individuals, spirituality supplies significance and a sense of comfort. It also provides meaning and a basis for decision making.

Researchers theorize that there are two primary reasons spiritual individuals live longer than others. The first is that regularly attending a faith community provides a sense of belonging and a safety net so individuals don't have to face life's difficulties alone.

Secondly, spirituality provides a moral code that makes people far less likely to engage in high risk, life-ending behaviors. The bottom line is that those who are spiritual tend to refrain from doing harmful things.

2. Avoid throwing out the baby with the bath water. When wounded, it's easy to discard spirituality completely. Instead of giving up, find a healthy faith community where people are growing, kindness and encouragement are plentiful, and where you don't have to be perfect to feel welcomed and valued.

Key indicators you've found a healthy community include that you aren't manipulated by shame and guilt, it's okay to say no and your spirituality, behavior and growth aren't micromanaged. Search until you find a healthy community. They exist.

3. Work through Steps 4, 5, 6 and 7 of Alcoholics Anonymous with someone you trust. Do this in private with an individual you are absolutely certain will not break your confidence. Let forgiveness free you from the chains that hold you back.

4. Heal old wounds. If you've been wounded by toxic faith, I encourage you to let go of the past and move forward as graciously as possible. Using "I" statements, say what you need to say and do what you need to do.

If you're carrying around bitterness and resentment, terminate or reposition a church and individuals who are unready, unwilling or unable to work through problems with you.

Lastly, do everything within your power to forgive those who wounded you, not for their sake, but so that you are freed to accept forgiveness and to move forward.

5. Remember that people and institutions will let you down. Not because they are malicious, though some are, but because everyone messes up. No one is perfect or unfailingly kind. Neither are you.

> *You'll never find a flawless spiritual community, but healthy ones do exist.*

6. Seek answers for yourself. Your spiritual journey is yours; so don't just rely on what you've heard others say. Seek for truth diligently, read spiritual works and pray for guidance in your search.

7. Find people who exude joy. Pay attention to individuals who, despite life's circumstances stay anchored and emanate peace, hope and joy. When you find such an individual, ask about the source of their joy.

Pick

My dear friend, Barb, radiates peace, hope and joy despite a lifetime of loss. Her dad was an abusive alcoholic and her mother committed suicide. She suffered the betrayal of an unfaithful spouse, worked four jobs to raise her son, battles a chronic illness and has grandchildren with health concerns.

Ask her how she's managed to survive and continue to thrive and she happily shares the source of her strength: Her close, personal relationship with Christ.

If you long for more, desire lasting peace, hope and joy and want to be free to live life to the fullest, I urge you to seek until you find the answers that satisfy your soul.

Pick to seek.

Pick to find.

Pick to live with peace, hope and joy.

Chapter 14

Little or Large:
How Big Are Your
Dreams?

"It is difficult to say what is impossible, for the dream of
yesterday is the hope of today and the reality of tomorrow."
                                                    Phillip Adams

Eighth grade. School magazine sales. A chance to win an
all-expense paid trip to Europe. I wanted it so badly I
could taste it.

The directions were clear, "In order to enter, you
must sell a Reader's Digest subscription."

Marching orders in hand, I approached my mom.
"No dear, Grandpa gives us a subscription every year."
Undaunted, I canvassed the neighborhood.

No interest.

Pick

Unwilling to give up, I widened my circle and began knocking at physician offices. The answer remained the same, "No, thanks."

Time, like grains of hour glass sand, was running out.

I kept trying.

"Would you like to order a copy of Reader's Digest?" I asked Dr. Brown, "I'm trying to win a trip to Europe."

I don't know if he wanted a copy. He may just have had a soft spot for a kid with her heart on her sleeve. "I'd love one," he replied.

Single subscription in hand, I went to the assistant principal's office. "Pick a form," said Mr. Mohler fanning out a stack of white papers. "If Pegasus is beneath the silver dot, you get to submit a 25 word essay on what you'd learn from a trip to Europe. If he's not, you're out."

"Please, Lord, let me pick a horse." Tentatively I reached out my hand and made my selection wondering if "eeny meeny miny moe" would have helped.

I immediately tried to wash the dot off with spit. Not very ladylike, but I needed to know. The silver dot smudged, darkening the paper. It was a scratch off.

"Please, please, please Lord."

Hands shaking, I gently rubbed it with a dime. I was terrified I'd tear it. Straining to see what lay beneath I caught a glimpse. There he was the mythical, winged horse.

"I got it! I got Pegasus!" I exclaimed to no one in particular. I couldn't wait to get home.

While excited for me, my parents didn't want me to get my hopes too high. "Kids all across the country sold

Reader's Digest this fall." I refused to be daunted. That trip was mine.

We sat around brainstorming and bantering ideas back and forth like a badminton birdie. There's only so much you can say in 25 words or less.

While too many years have passed for me to remember the entire essay, I do remember the last half. "Winning this trip will make me a better citizen of my town, country and world."

Having done everything within my power, I again asked God to grant me my dream and sent it off.

Months passed with deafening silence, but my dream never faltered. I even turned down an invitation to compete in a gymnastics meet, "I think I'll be in Europe."

"All junior high students please report to the auditorium," boomed the loud speaker.

Grateful to get out of class, hundreds of adolescents converged on the lobby. We jostled for entry.

The moment I stepped inside, I saw the man from Reader's Digest. Heart leaping like a flame I whispered to my best friend, "Someone from here won that trip."

Barely able to breathe, I waited, heart pounding like a big bass drum.

"I'll die if someone else wins it."

Polite applause greeted our guest, then silence. He thanked us for making the magazine sale a huge success. My only thought was, "Get to the point."

Pick

"Over 13,000 students from across the United States entered our contest," he began. "We selected seventeen winners. One is from Dover."

He paused for dramatic effect.

I perched on the edge of my seat, eyes unblinking, heart strings taut. "The winner is Sherene McHenry." Shaking and shocked, I made my way to the stage.

My dream came true.

My world got bigger.

My heart grew bolder.

I learned many things that year. First and foremost that big, audacious dreams really can come true.

> *Big dreams really*
> *can come true.*

I also learned dreams need feet. Pegasus didn't fly into my lap. I knocked on door after door repeatedly encountering rejection. The trip to Europe was the desire of my heart. As such, I was unwilling to give up when faced with repeated refusals.

When it comes to dreaming, I can only do my part. In this case I needed to sell a subscription and write the best essay I possibly could. Then, with a wing and a prayer I had to turn the outcome of my dream over to others. There are things outside of my control.

Finally, I learned firsthand that daring to dream something so close to my heart made me extremely vulnerable. I was either going to be ecstatic if it came true or crushed if it didn't. When a dream really matters, there's no in between.

Telling the story transports me to the same spot emotionally. Even after all these years, my chest still constricts and my eyes brim with tears as I re-experience wanting something so badly it physically hurt. There have been few things in life I've wanted more.

Fast forward 30 years. Just as in eighth grade, I put my heart on the line hoping and aching for another dream to come true.

As long as I can remember I wanted to live at the lake. I love the water. Speed boats and jet skis make me giggle. Even more than that, I long for the peace that nature provides my soul.

I found a house with an incredible view. My desk would look out at the lake. I would be inspired to write. I wanted it. Badly.

Kelley, a dear friend, drove out with me to see it. Sharing my hopes with her on the top of the stairs leading down to the dock, my eyes welled with tears. My breath flittered in my throat like a butterfly. It was eighth grade all over again.

Would God again answer the prayers of my heart? Would He let me live somewhere so beautiful?

Graciously, He once again gave me my heart's desire. As I write, I look out on water that is ever changing. Contentment fills my soul.

Pick

Before you're tempted to think I get everything I want, there have been dreams close to my heart that haven't, and never will, come true.

The most painful was my desire to have children.

I waited for the right man to sweep me off my feet.

He never came.

I waited longer.

Time marched on.

The window closed.

I mourned the passing of my dream.

On occasion, I still do.

Any way you slice it, it hurts when heartfelt dreams don't materialize. The good news is we humans are a resilient bunch. As such, my dream has shifted to hoping to marry someone with kids. Until then, I enjoy other people's children. I love my nieces and nephew. I move forward.

While I don't always get to say if my dreams come true, I do get to pick my response. When I focus on the good things I've been granted, I'm happy. When I key in on what my life lacks, misery moves in. The choice is mine.

I'm sure you've heard the saying *it's better to have loved and lost than never to have loved.* The same applies to dreams. Even greater than the pain of dashed desire is the dull ache of regret and "what could have been."

What about you? Do you dare to dream the audacious? Do you ever open your heart to wanting something so badly it hurts?

Or do you struggle to identify what you want? Have the decades deadened your dreams? Have you encountered too many disappointments along life's way? Were you taught that it's selfish to want things? That dreams are for other people? That you should be happy with what you have?

How much and how big you dream depends largely on your personality, how many times your heart has been crushed, and what you learned in childhood. I'm blessed to have parents who continually told me, "There isn't anything you can't do as long as you put your mind to it and are willing to work hard."

I believed them. Still do.

In addition, my dad, a dreamer himself, repeatedly encouraged me to have lofty ambitions and to go after what I wanted. Knowing that pain is a price of dreaming, he'd gently say, "Dreamers get hurt sometimes." Nodding, we'd both agree that the opportunity for joy was well worth the risk of possible pain.

Along with the possibility of great joy, dreaming invites the possibility of immense pain.

Others grow up in far different environments, like a former student who got stuck when assigned to generate a list of 25 things she'd like to have, be or do in a career class.

"I don't have any dreams," she matter-of-factly stated.

"No dreams?" I countered.

"No."

"Not even one?" I queried with confusion.

"No. I don't have any dreams," she answered flatly.

Pick

"Well, do you want to pass the class?" I asked.

"Yes."

"That's one."

"Hoping to graduate?"

"Of course," she answered emphatically.

"You're up to two," I grinned.

She wasn't amused.

As we talked further she told me that she used to love to sing. One day, as a little girl she was invited to perform on The Lawrence Welk Show, yesteryear's American Idol.

Her parents said no.

In response, she shut off part of her soul.

"Dreams just lead to pain," she explained. "It's better not to hope than to hurt."

My heart broke for the little girl whose dreams were dashed. And all the years that followed.

Life lived in gray.

Safe. Predictable. Mundane.

No sharp pangs of pain, but lacking hope and joy.

> *A life without dreams is*
> *a life without joy.*

In case you're wondering, she did generate her list, earned an A in the class and graduated with her master's degree in counseling. Not too shabby for a little girl who quit dreaming.

Whether you regularly dare to dream the audacious or if your wings were clipped long ago, you can awaken and strengthen your ability to dreamy:

Little or Large

1. **If you aren't already aware, get to know what you like and what brings you joy.** Comb through your life like a treasure seeker using a metal detector. Activities, things and people you enjoy emanate an internal buzz of delight.

Like a farmer who turns the soil in preparation for planting, as you key into the things that make you happy and stir your soul, you naturally awaken your dreams and desires.

2. **Generate a top 100 things you want to have, be or do list.** Yes, 100. The twenty-five I assigned my students was a teaser. You cared enough to purchase a book on how to create a life you love. You can do it.

The point of generating a Top 100 list is to open yourself to possibilities and the longings of your heart. Your list can center on career, family, relationships, travel, possessions, financial or spiritual things and any other category you desire.

Live on the wild side as you create your bucket list. Forget about practicality or whether or not you think something is possible, selfish, or too mundane. Just find a quiet place, open your heart and dream away.

> *It's amazing what will bubble up if you slow down long enough and allow yourself to truly think, feel and dream.*

Nearly two decades ago, after reading Barbara Sher's *Wishcraft*, I generated my own top 100 list. Wading out 20 feet, I perched on a rock in Lake Michigan, waves playfully tickling my feet. The memory brings a smile to my face.

151

Pick

My list ranged from not wanting a mini-lake in my backyard when it rained due to a drainage problem, to having three strands of real pearls and a set of Christmas china, to being an international bestselling author.

Remarkably, as Sher promised, many of my dreams came true with little or no effort on my part. I don't even remember writing down one of my favorites, "Go to the theatre in London."

About a decade ago, Mom and I took a lovely trip to London, overdosed on shows and even got upgraded to first class on the flight over. The only letdown was flying coach on the trip home. Talk about spoiled.

I pull out my list every couple of years to see my progress. It's amazing how many of my dreams have check marks and dates documenting when they came true. Some, like my dreams surrounding the type of person I want to be and what I want to accomplish during my time on earth, are works in progress.

Others have yet to be realized.

I remain optimistic.

Still others, like my desire to have 35 million dollars by the time I was 35, never will. While it would have been lovely, I haven't once bemoaned that dream not coming true. Additionally, as I haven't shot a bow and arrow since childhood, my failure to win Olympic gold in archery hasn't been troubling.

Not winning a teaching excellence award was far more difficult to swallow.

Realizing that people and dreams change over time, I've made my Top 100 list twice. Once I finish *Pick*, I believe I'll generate a third list.

> *It never hurts to have 100*
> *dreams in the hopper.*

What about you? If you could have, do or be anything, what would you desire? What's on your bucket list?

3. Get crystal clear about what you want. Now that you've generated your list, I'm sure you can see the things you've listed aren't equally important. That's a good thing. It would not be humanly impossible to give focused and sustained energy to 100 dreams at the same time.

Like Sher, I believe that many things on your list will naturally happen with little or no effort on your part. Attribute it to what you will; I personally believe God is a big God who delights in giving good things. At the same time, the dreams that matter, those closest to your heart, almost always take sustained effort to achieve.

Prioritize what's important to you, paying particular attention to the one or two dreams that truly generate your excitement and enthusiasm. These are your passion points. Powerful and compelling, they point to your true purpose and are deserving of everything you have to give them.

I love helping people develop healthier relationships and happier lives. I also get jazzed about speaking and writing. It makes sense that one of my top dreams is to be a highly paid, highly sought after, international bestselling author and speaker.

Pick

My sister, on the other hand, has dreamed of being a full-time mom from the time she was a child. As she proofread *Pick* she said, "Makes me feel like I need to get out there and do something with my life."

"You're living your dream." I reminded her. "You're a full-time mom."

I couldn't be more proud of her. Although her life isn't always easy and at the end of every day she's bone tired, she's the happiest mother I've ever seen.

Sure, they could have more material things if she worked outside the home, but things have never been her primary dream. My sister simply wants to raise her own children. Prioritizing, sacrificing and working together, she and her husband turned her lifelong dream into their reality.

What about you? What dreams matter most to you? What dream is so close to your heart that you cannot bear to give up or fail?

I don't know your dream. Maybe it's to champion social justice, lower the divorce rate, change the life of troubled youth, ease the suffering of others or find the cure for AIDS.

Perhaps you dream of being a performer, writing children's books or becoming an FBI agent. Maybe you dream of working outdoors, climbing mountains, traveling to all seven continents or creating a fantastic marriage.

Whether you know exactly what your dream is or if you're still seeking, you have one. You were put on this planet, at this time, for a reason. Find that reason.

*Your talents and treasures
are needed.*

4. If you're married or have children, encourage each family member to compile a Top 25 list. Wonderful discussions will ensue as you share your hearts. The only rules are to compile the list on your own and not to belittle or ridicule someone else's dreams. Once you know what others long for, you can work as a family to help make each other's dreams come true.

Once you've identified each individual's dreams, working together, create a Top 10 list for your family. Doing so will provide you with a blueprint for how to best invest your family's energies and resources.

How to spend family time becomes clearer.

Vacation planning becomes easier.

Budgeting becomes less painful.

My hope is that you will give voice to the whispers of your heart. That you will dare to dream the audacious. That you will take time to figure out your purpose and passion.

Whether clear or still formulating, your dreams matter and are worth pursuing. The world is full of possibilities.

Pick to risk.

Pick to dream.

Pick to receive.

Chapter 15

Dreamer or Doer: Turn Your Dreams Into Realities

"When people say to me: 'How do you do so many things?' I often answer them without meaning to be cruel: 'How do you do so little?' It seems to me that people have vast potential. Most people can do extraordinary things if they have the confidence or take the risks. Yet most people sit in front of the TV and treat life as if it goes on forever."

Phillip Adams

I've long held lofty dreams. That part comes easily for me. Transitioning from dreamer to doer on the other hand, has been an extremely difficult journey.

Spoiled by having so many of the desires of my heart materialize with little or no apparent effort on my part, I

Pick

bought the lie. You know the one. All you need for your dreams to come true is to believe strongly enough and wait patiently enough.

So I dreamed.

I would fill arenas offering help, hope and healing to audiences around the globe.

I would write books translated into 28 languages.

I would marry Mr. Wonderful.

I would lose weight.

I would own a boat and jet skis.

And I waited.

Patiently.

Undaunted, I waited even longer.

Then longer still.

Months turned into years then slid silently into decades. Ever waiting for my dearest dreams to come true:

I bemoaned my lack of progress.

I grew discouraged.

I became confused.

What was wrong with me?

Why weren't my dreams coming true?

I held on by a string.

"It's a good thing I'm an optimist," I'd say saddened and chagrined. "Otherwise I'd have given up long ago." The truth was my dreams were too precious for me to give up. I couldn't bear to abandon them.

Pick is a prime example of my struggles. Having started this book over a decade ago, "I'm still working on it" has long been an embarrassing answer.

I've had every reason to finish *Pick*. It's what I eat, sleep and breathe. I've presold copies. It will change lives and families. It will expand my reach, help my career and provide income. I even like to write.

Yet I've struggled to finish it. Why have I struggled so? What has kept me from finishing *Pick* and achieving the dreams closest to my heart?

Rhonda Britton, author of *Do I Look Fat In This,* shed light on one of my primary problems: *magical thinking.* I mistakenly believed that something I wanted or needed was going to happen without my active participation.

Relief flooded me.

I had a label. All that was holding me back from living my dreams was magical thinking.

I accepted her invitation to start telling myself the truth and to actively engage in pursuing the things I wanted. My mantra became, "No more magical thinking about boys, toys, weight, writing or speaking." I said it over and over as I walked the neighborhood.

Instead of simply waiting for Prince Charming to show up, jet skis and a boat to magically materialize, thinking I'd lose weight without any effort on my part and that my speaking and writing career would simply take off, I changed how I thought.

No results. I was just as stuck with my catchy mantra as without. Something was still missing.

"I don't know why I can't make my dreams come true," I lamented to my mastermind group. "What's wrong with me? Should I go to another speaking or writing conference? What about a conference on success? Maybe I need to hire a life coach. I don't know what to do."

"Come with me to Mark LeBlanc's Small Business Success Seminar," invited Eleni, a dear friend who speaks professionally. "I think he'll be just what you need."

Willing to give anything a try, I booked my flight that day. Eleni was right. Working with Mark has changed my life professionally and personally.

The most important thing Mark taught me is that if I want to turn my dreams into realities, I need to take deliberate and consistent action. Very similar to the part of Britton's formula I had conveniently overlooked when I created my mantra: to actively engage in pursuing the things I wanted.

> *The secret to achieving dreams is to move from magical thinking to deliberate and consistent action.*

Mark's secret to success is to engage in three high value activities (HVAs) a day. I can almost hear you, "OK, three HVAs. What's an HVA?"

An HVA is any action that moves you step by baby step ever closer to achieving your dream.

Just as dreams differ, so do HVAs. For example, if your dream is to be a great parent or spouse your HVAs will revolve around promoting healthy relationships and creating an environment that works for you and your family.

If your dream is to go to college or earn an advanced degree, your HVAs will encompass steps towards getting into and finishing an academic program.

If your dream is to be debt free, your HVAs will revolve around setting and keeping a budget, paying down existing debt and setting aside savings.

Notice that LeBlanc doesn't advocate grand efforts as HVAs. Grand gestures simply aren't sustainable day after day. Just three baby steps every day, day after day, until you achieve your dream.

Examples of HVAs that, step by baby step, move me ever closer to my dreams include such things as writing for 30 minutes, spending 15 minutes on marketing materials and making a business call.

Three HVAs a day.

Deceptively simple.

Decidedly difficult.

I did great on my HVAs for the first six months, making more progress toward my dreams than in the previous 15 years combined. The forward momentum was intoxicating. Excitement oozed from every pore.

Then, slowly I began to taper off and missed an HVA here or there. *No big deal,* I thought. I was still going gangbusters and hitting at least two HVAs every day.

Then the inevitable happened. Missed singular HVAs turned into days without a single HVA. You can guess what happened next, I didn't do an HVA for an entire week. Then, before I knew it, I had missed multiple months.

Like a car running out of gas, my forward motion slowed then faltered. My progress towards achieving my dreams ground to a screeching halt.

Pick

I didn't intend to derail or delay my dreams. I had viable excuses. I was sick, I was tired, a project came up, I just didn't feel like doing them...

I started saying, "I'll do my HVAs after I watch TV." Yeah, right. My ability to lie knew no bounds.

"I'll do them tomorrow."

As a child I once heard my father tell a man, "tomorrow never comes." He's right, tomorrow never comes for dreamers who haven't figured out how to be doers.

> *Dreams without action remain dreams.*

Natural born doers on the other hand don't struggle with the tendency to put off until tomorrow what needs to be done today.

Take my niece, Danie. She, like other doers, determines what she wants, maps out her strategy for success and begins to march towards her objective.

Regardless of conditions she unrelentingly moves forward. Rain doesn't rattle her. Blizzards are merely inconvenient. Heat hardens her resolve.

I didn't recognize her doer mindset until she got sick and spent the better part of her high school years hospitalized. Despite circumstances and overwhelming odds, she steadfastly proclaimed, "I'm going to graduate on time."

I couldn't see it happening, but I didn't have the heart to squelch her dream. I'd nod and say, "I love your dream and willingness to work hard to achieve it."

Dreamer or Doer

A driven doer, Danie studied and took the extra class she needed to graduate her senior year. Achieving her dream, she graduated on time.

Along the way, she never wavered from her desire to be a nurse. Unfortunately, Danie went to a university where only 10% of applicants are accepted into the nursing program. Being a doer, Danie had a plan.

"I'm going to work hard and get in. If I don't, I'll transfer to another school." Countless hours of dedicated study resulted in a 3.89 GPA and an acceptance letter.

Her first job was in an intensive care unit. "This is really good," she explained. "You need trauma experience if you want to be a nurse anesthetist. I'm going to work and study all year, take my GRE's and start applying to graduate schools. If I don't get in, I'll reapply until I do."

"Sounds great," I replied. "Just make sure you really know what the job entails." It's hard for someone with a background in career counseling not to give advice.

Danie interviewed nurse anesthetists, visited work sites and engaged in job shadowing. Her interest and determination grew. "It's exactly what I want to do," she'd exclaim excitedly.

One thing she learned is how hard it is to get into nurse anesthetist programs. Hundreds of highly qualified applicants apply for coveted spots every year. Rigorous interviews narrow the field down to the chosen few.

She started by applying to three schools and got invited to three day-long interviews. She found herself far younger than the other interviewees. She also had far fewer credentials.

Although intimidated, Danie hung in there, "At least I'll be prepared for next year's interviews."

Drum roll please. Danie the doer got accepted into multiple programs and is working diligently to complete her studies. What an incredible achievement in the face of overwhelming odds.

> *Doers get things done.*

What about you? Are you making steady progress towards your dreams? Or are you engaging in magical thinking, doing little if anything yet all the while hoping and believing your dreams will "someday" come true?

Don't be hard on yourself if you've been living in the land of magical thinking. Since you were young, you've heard of a fairy godmother swooping in, sprinkling a little bibideebobideeboo and without any effort on her part, Cinderella was beautiful for the ball.

Perhaps you're a doer when it comes to dreams, but there are other important areas of your life where you're engaging in magical thinking.

For example, do you have financial or work problems you aren't addressing, but you keep hoping they'll go away? Do you have a troubled relationship you're trusting will get better on its own? Is there something you want to buy but aren't saving up to purchase?

Dreamer or Doer

Magical thinking is extremely detrimental to being happy and living life to the fullest. It puts you on the sidelines, a bystander with no say in your destiny.

> *Magical thinking leads to*
> *frustration and failure.*

The following are tips to help you move from dreamer to doer:

1. **Resolve today to move beyond magical thinking.** No more believing that "someday" your dream is going to magically materialize without consistent and deliberate effort on your part. You've heard the saying, "If it's to be it's up to me." Apply that adage to achieving your dreams and you're well on your way.

> *Move beyond dreaming*
> *into doing.*

2. **Engage in three HVAs every day.** You are the captain of your ship. It's up to you to claim your destiny by engaging in three HVAs a day.

Begin by deciding what it is that you want to achieve and map out what it will take for you to get there by a realistic date. Then consistently take three baby steps each and every day that move you ever closer to your dream.

Not as sexy, easy or quick as magical thinking, but ever so much more effective. It's amazing how much better things work out for me when I do three HVAs a day. You'll find the same to be true.

Pick

I estimate that before I worked with Mark I engaged in about 25 to 50 HVAs a year. Implementing three HVAs a day, I now accomplish more in a month than I used to get done in a year—even devoting Sundays to rejuvenation. As a result, dreams that used to only exist on a distant horizon have come true.

3. **Realize that consistency matters.** Like Aesop's tortoise and the hare, consistency wins the race. When you choose to deliberately engage in three HVAs daily, you set yourself up for sustainable success.

> *Think about the progress you'll make if you take three steps towards your dream a day, 90 steps a month and more than 1,000 steps a year.*
> *Mark LeBlanc*

One of my major roadblocks in finishing *Pick* has been inconsistency. For years I only wrote when I felt like it. Riding the inspiration wave, I'd hammer out text for hours exhausting both brain and body. The only problem was, it would take me at least six months to recover from my writing binge and get back to work.

I felt like the instructions on a shampoo bottle:

Lather. Rinse. Repeat.

Write. Burn myself out. Repeat.

I experienced just enough forward motion to keep me hopeful, but nowhere near enough to actually finish the book. I began to doubt my ability to fulfill my dream.

Long before working with Mark, I attended a writing workshop. There I learned that individuals who write anywhere from 15 minutes to three hours a day, every day, are far more prolific than those who write sporadically.

When you add in accountability, productivity skyrockets.

"I prefer to write when inspired," I explained to Elizabeth afterwards. "It's how I'm wired." Then off I'd go and burn myself out again.

Sometimes wisdom seeps in slowly.

Consistency
wins the race.

4. Make your HVAs small, doable baby steps, not grand gestures. Writing for 30 minutes a day is a doable HVA for me. Writing for a day or finishing a chapter isn't sustainable for me. Think small steps and set yourself up for success.

When I make my HVAs too big, I quickly grind to a halt and begin generating excuses. Then I start feeling like a failure which further decreases my energy and drive and all of the sudden, I'm off the HVA bandwagon watching TV.

HVAs become burdensome
when they get too big.

Mark taught me to keep my HVAs achievable. As he's fond of reminding me, "You can always write longer than half an hour, Sherene. Success breeds success. All it takes is three small baby steps each and every day."

5. Employ an internal accountability measure. If you're a dreamer, you already know it can be difficult to keep motivated and moving over the long haul. Distractions and discouragement derail dreamers. The antidote to getting off track is accountability.

Set yourself up for success by creating an internal accountability system and using it religiously. I highly recommend creating an HVA log and keeping it open on your desk. Each morning write out the three HVAs you will engage in that day. At the end of the day, put a "Y" signifying "yes, I did it" by each completed HVA.

When I was going full guns, my HVA log sat open on my desk. Every morning I wrote down the three baby steps I would complete that day. At the end of each day I put my "Y" next to each completed HVA.

I quickly fell in love with my "Ys". I also felt great. Mark is right, success generates success. Each day I marked off three completed HVAs, my energy and excitement grew. So did my productivity and progress towards my dreams.

My downward spiral began when I stopped keeping my HVA log out in plain sight. I kept it in my purse and would pull it out on occasion. After a while I quit keeping it all together. It was then that I went from missing days to missing weeks to missing months. Today my HVA journal once again sits out on my desk.

Your HVA log will enable you to tell yourself the truth about what you are and aren't doing and help you hold yourself accountable. Just as dieters who journal everything become increasingly mindful of what they are eating, individuals who keep HVA logs are able to hold themselves far more accountable than those who don't.

6. Utilize external accountability. External accountability entails reporting what you've done to someone else. For example, Mark is my business coach and when I was going gangbusters, I sent him monthly accountability reports.

Pulling together my numbers helped me tell myself the truth and keep on track. Numbers also helped Mark best help me during our coaching sessions. When I quit sending in my numbers and stopped booking regular sessions, my productivity and profitability plummeted.

I'm back on board. Working regularly with Mark keeps me on track, significantly cuts down my learning curve and helps me move more quickly when I get stuck.

One of the other things I really appreciate is that in addition to telling me the truth and holding me accountable for my actions, Mark also encourages me. He consistently refocuses me, helps me set realistic goals and conveys his belief in me. What a priceless resource.

If you are serious about achieving your dreams, get serious about being accountable and find someone to whom you can report your progress on a monthly basis.

Pick someone you respect, someone who is honest and someone who believes in you. The right person might be a member of your professional association, a business or life coach or a member of your faith community.

Whomever you choose, they need to be willing to:

Pick

- Have you report in on a consistent basis.
- Celebrate your achievements and progress.
- Encourage you.
- Tell you the truth.
- Let you go if you insist on wasting their time.

Don't ask your parent, best friend or coworker to be your accountability person, and under no circumstances ask your spouse. Doing so will upset the ever so delicate balance in your relationships.

Don't become your spouse's accountability partner either. They married you because they wanted a loving spouse, not a coach, teacher or parent.

Additionally, don't ask a friend who uses you in turn for accountability. It becomes far too easy to make excuses and let each other off the hook.

If you're willing to tell yourself and another human being the truth about what you've done, external accountability will work wonders for you. While you may be willing to make excuses for yourself or wallow in disgust about what you haven't done, you won't want to repeatedly look bad to another person.

> *External accountability*
> *is a great motivator.*

Whether it's lofty or small, world altering or simply personally fulfilling, your dream matters. Sadly, the world is full of dreamers who never move beyond dreaming. Actively pursuing and achieving your dream will change you, your world and the world around you.

  Pick to be powerful.

  Pick to be productive.

  Pick to do and make your dreams come true.

Chapter 16

Reactive or Proactive: Rise Above Resistance

"Keep away from people who try to belittle your ambitions. Small people always do that, but the really great make you feel that you, too, can become great."

Mark Twain

When I announced I was quitting my job to speak, write and consult, people's responses were all over the board.

Some were excited, cheering me on and affirming my ability to succeed. "You can do it." "You were made to do this." "You need to do what you love and love what you do." "It's about time."

Others were concerned. Making such a change in a down economy seemed foolhardy and reckless.

"The economy is bad."

Pick

"You have better benefits than anyone I know."

"Do you have any idea what insurance costs?"

"It's not the best time to leave a secure job."

"You have a job that people envy."

"Can't you be content with what you have?"

Far more painful were the escalating attacks about my character, the questioning of my work ethic and the sabotaging of a program I'd labored years to build. The silent treatment shouted my isolation.

The months leading up to my transition were upsetting. I cried. More than once.

I'm not the first, nor will I be the last, person to encounter resistance. Consider Tiffany, a high school senior I mentored from a rough, underprivileged, chaotic background. Her father was absent and had been most of her life. Poverty plagued, her mother struggled to keep a roof over their heads and to make meager ends meet.

Tiffany was left to fend for herself. It was up to her to decide when to go to bed, what to eat and whether or not to attend school. Despite daily distress, Tiffany dreamed of being the first person in her family to graduate from high school.

Like a distance runner rounding the final corner, the finish line was in Tiffany's sight. She just needed to complete her senior year. However, Tiffany's daring to reach for what no one in her family had achieved activated a steady flow of resistance that grew with every passing week.

Her mother and older sister led the charge. Each comment, temptation and disruption designed to derail success.

"You study all the time."

"Take a break and have some fun."

"I know it's a school night, but come out with us."

"The car isn't working. You'll have to miss school."

"Mom needs you, you can't abandon her."

"You have to work."

"You think you're better than the rest of us."

"All you ever think about is yourself."

"How can you be so selfish?"

"You know you're never going to amount to anything."

"Even if you do finish high school, you'll never go to college."

Like a castle under the assault of a battering ram, Tiffany's dream was continually attacked. She cried. She got angry. She even laughed at some of their antics. Weary of the fight, she considered giving up.

"What's the point?" she questioned more than once.

Firmly believing that education is a ticket out of poverty, I shared statistics about how much more she would earn over the course of her life, even more if she finished college. I also reminded her of the advantages it would give her children should she ever choose to have them.

While I was able to listen to Tiffany's frustration and confusion, provide a voice of reason and help her keep her eye on the prize, Tiffany was the one who had to face and fight the resistance.

Although it was tough, Tiffany held on and ultimately achieved her dream. Her persistence changed the course of her life. It also opened a door of hope to those who followed her. Once one person takes a risk and breaks a barrier, it's far easier for others to do the same.

Watching Tiffany's family try to keep her from achieving her dream and facing my own resistance taught me a great deal.

I learned that happy individuals who pursue their own hopes and dreams tend to be extremely supportive of others taking chances and choosing to create a life they love. Brave risk takers themselves, they encourage and help others keep their eye on the prize.

Conversely, I also discovered the most exaggerated resistance comes from unhappy individuals failing to pursue their own hopes and dreams.

It's far easier to take jabs at someone else than it is to take risks and do the hard work of creating a desirable life. The bottom line is, if they can keep others from reaching their dreams, they're able to remain comfortable with their own life choices.

> *People are a lot like crabs. When a crab tries to climb out of a pail, the others repeatedly thwart escape attempts by grabbing it and pulling it back down.*

Opposition needs to be anticipated when the boat gets rocked. Whether someone is reaching for their dreams or simply setting a boundary, they can expect to encounter escalating resistance from friends, family and coworkers.

People desire stability and balance. They have a vested interest in things staying the same. When someone chooses to change and reach for more, it threatens and disrupts others.

Resistance is the norm,
not the exception.

Fear and anger also activate attacks. Change can create great fear and anger in others and lead to highly predictable, ever escalating attacks.

Most resistance starts with a warning shot across the bow in the form of a question or suggestion. "You need to do what's best for you, but have you considered…"

If the warning shot works and you back down and give up your dream, they go on their merry way having easily won the battle.

If you don't back down, you can expect the questions and suggestions to become increasingly more pointed and controlling. "You really need to look at …"

If you don't give in and go back to behaving the way you always behaved, their attacks will intensify and become increasingly personal. "You think you're so much better than everyone else…" "You're so selfish…"

If those attacks don't work, you can expect to be on the receiving end of explosive anger, the silent treatment or character assassination. They may also threaten to sever the relationship, "If you do that, the relationship is over," or "I'll never forgive you."

Having expected you to capitulate long ago, the attacker will grab at anything in their final attempts to get you to back down.

The good news is, if an individual is healthy and loves you, they will recover and their resistance will subside. Even if sticking to your guns freaks someone out, most of the time if you hang on tight and weather out the storm, they'll come around. They may even eventually take credit for your life changing decision.

What about you? Do you feel guilty for chasing a dream or wanting more? Do you wonder if the guilt you feel will ever go away?

Are you fearful of the wrath of others? Have you been punished for wanting and pursuing more? Are you being beaten down by attacks designed to hold you back? Do you feel manipulated into giving in to other's expectations? Are you afraid your relationships will be damaged beyond repair?

If you desire to be better equipped to face resistance and move past the pain and guilt such resistance evokes, you are not alone. Choosing to create a life you love takes a great deal of courage. It's far easier, albeit far less satisfying, to stay with the status quo.

The following are tips and suggestions to help you overcome the adversity and resistance that will arise when you choose to reach higher and create a life you love:

1. Follow dreams that matter. Chasing a dream that matters enables you to stay the course despite fatigue and fierce resistance. If you're not passionate about your dream or can't see how it matters, get yourself a better, bigger dream. Believing in something larger than yourself will empower you to persevere despite opposition.

2. Visualize achieving your dream. A dream that positively changes your life and the lives of those around you is worth clinging to for dear life. When you're tempted to think it isn't worth the grief, pain or struggle, picture yourself having completed your dream.

Feel your success, the extent of your dream's impact and envision the rewards that will accompany your accomplishment. Doing so will renew your will to press on.

I regularly remind myself of the lives, including my own, that will be touched with *Pick*. I picture myself in front of crowds who need help getting from point A to point B, and I often remind myself of the rewards that await me upon its completion. Visualizing *Pick's* impact and rewards keeps me writing when I'd rather be playing.

> *Keep your eye*
> *on the prize.*

3. Recognize resistance isn't always about you. While it may feel like it, resistance isn't always about you and what you're trying to achieve. It's about how chasing dreams and setting boundaries evokes fear, resentment and anger in others.

Pick

Put yourself into their shoes in order to better understand their perspective. Tiffany's mom and sister were embarrassed they hadn't finished high school. They didn't want to feel bad about their choices or to be reminded that they could have graduated if they'd been willing to delay gratification and tough it out.

4. **Reframe resistance.** It's hard to hear bad things about yourself when attacks turn personal. It's also difficult to have dreams dashed. View resistance as an indicator that you are changing, growing and working to create a life you love.

> *You can tell how much you've changed*
> *by how hard people try to keep you*
> *as you've always been.*
> *Dr. Brenda Freeman*

5. **When in doubt, check it out.** While it's important to be open to feedback, not all comments are valid or helpful. If you're being told how terrible you are or encountering other painful, confusing and doubt provoking resistance, reality check the flack you're getting with a gentle truth teller, counselor or life coach.

I can't tell you how often I've asked, "Am I out to lunch?"

I am profoundly grateful for the gentle truth tellers in my life. Sometimes they say yes, but most often they laugh at the absurdity of the dagger designed to dampen my dreams. In doing so they set me straight and empower me to press on.

Reactive or Proactive

Boundaries are a primary defense against resistance. If you want to create a life you love and live your dreams, you must set appropriate boundaries.

When encountering resistance, be it mocking, belittling or sabotaging, ask them to stop. Let their response guide you in deciding how much access you allow them to your time, talent and treasures.

If they are respectful and willing to change, keep them in the loop. If not, limit the topics you discuss, as well as, the time you spend with anyone unwilling to modify negative behaviors. When you set and hold boundaries with kindness, you may be pleasantly surprised with what happens.

> *It's up to you to protect your time and emotional energy.*

6. Remember guilt goes away, resentment grows. There will be times you feel guilty about following your dreams. Your alternative is to give up and live a lesser life. That's when resentment creeps in. As stated previously, it's helpful to remember that guilt goes away while resentment grows and eats away life satisfaction.

> *Guilt goes away, resentment builds.*

At the end of the day, dummying down or giving up on your dreams doesn't improve your quality of life or help make the world a better place. When you refuse to succumb

Pick

to resistance and strive for your dreams in spite of it, you show others they too can create a life they love.

Pick to set boundaries.

Pick to persist.

Pick to achieve.

Chapter 17

Lollygag or Launch:
Get Going

"Do not live as though you had a thousand years before you."

Marcus Aurelius

Ten long years ago I started this book. Today I finish it. It's been quite a journey. Along the way I've experienced hope and despair, progress and delay, clarity and confusion. I've felt alone and I've felt supported. I've been excited and I've been exhausted. Only my desire to create a life I love and to live my dreams stayed constant.

Although *Pick* tells my story and I hope you'll learn from my mistakes and achieve your dreams far more quickly, *Pick* isn't about me. It's about you, your hopes and dreams and your ability to actively create a life you love.

You were designed to accomplish something significant with the time you've been given. Never allow yourself to forget that you are here for a purpose.

Pick

You will face obstacles, self-doubt and the ridicule of those who do not understand you or your dreams. Expect resistance, but don't let it define who you are or get in the way of creating a life you love.

There will be days when you're discouraged and tempted to give up. You'll self-sabotage and on occasion stall out. When you do, refuse to give up or to consider yourself a failure or a fraud. Dust yourself off and get back on track as quickly as possible.

Regularly remind yourself of the power and purpose of your dream. Persistence is key to creating a life you love. Giving up and magical thinking don't produce results. Awareness, acceptance, action and accountability do.

> *Believing strongly in the value of your dream and being crystal clear about what you want empowers you to persist despite discouragement, resistance and setbacks.*

Boundaries are your dream's best friend. Refuse to over and under-function. Say "yes" to things that are good and that you can do cheerfully. Say "no" to things that pull you away from your purpose and for which you have neither the time nor the resources. You are responsible for how you invest your time, talent and resources.

Be careful whom you let into your inner circle. Drainers, takers, players, liars and gators will zap your drive and diminish your ability to create a life you love.

Embrace parade and confetti throwers, gentle truth tellers, encouragers and individuals willing to work with you to create win-win solutions. As you consciously surround yourself with individuals who bring out the best in you and spur you on, you position yourself for success.

Keep focused on the facets in life over which you have control. Your energy is far too important to squander fretting over things you cannot change. Worrying will rob you of joy, energy and time and give you nothing of value in exchange.

De-clutter your life, emotionally and physically. You can ill afford to lug around the balls and chains that accompany both forms of clutter.

Work to develop an attitude of gratitude. Embrace happiness and spirituality and cultivate a strong sense of humor. Creating a life you love is hard work and can be physically and emotionally exhausting. Take time to regularly engage in activities that replenish your soul. Play.

When stressed or upset, turn to healthy coping strategies that add to your resiliency level and further fuel your ability to achieve your dreams.

Dare to dream and pursue the audacious—big dreams, dreams that matter, dreams that touch your heart, dreams that change the world. I love Carolyn Arrend's *Seize the Day*. In it she sings:

> *"One thing I've noticed wherever I wander*
> *Everyone's got a dream they can follow or squander,*
> *You can do what you will with the days you are given,*
> *I'm trying to spend mine on the business of living…*
> *Seize the day, seize whatever you can*
> *'Cause life slips away just like hourglass sand."*

Pick

Time is precious and passes ever so quickly. You alone determine if you will pursue your purpose and create a life you love, or if you'll resign yourself to living with regret and recrimination.

When you pursue your dreams with intention and integrity and care as much about others as you do for yourself, you're guaranteed to make the world a better place. Take action and make good decisions. When you mess up, regroup as quickly as possible, do what it takes to make things right and get back on track.

I believe in you and in the power of your purpose.

Pick to pursue your passions and dreams.

Pick to persevere despite difficulties.

Pick to create a life you love.

About the Author

Dr. Sherene McHenry founder of Fully Engaged, LLC, works with individuals and organizations who want their members to develop healthier relationships, avoid burnout and be more effective on a daily basis.

Passionate about helping others live life to the fullest, Sherene has spoken on three continents to a wide range of audiences. She's also helped businesses achieve record profits, been quoted in the Wall Street Journal, and is a former full professor at Central Michigan University where she trained counselors for almost two decades.

Sharing principles that work, Sherene combines the knowledge she gained earning her Ph.D. in Counselor Education at the University of Wyoming and experience as a Licensed Professional Counselor with a life full of trials and triumphs, hopes and dreams, and her fair share of blunders and bloopers. In addition to *Pick*, she is the author of *The Busy Student's Guide to College and Career Success*.

Sherene is a member of the National Speakers Association and serves as a board member of the National Speakers Association Michigan Chapter. She's also a member of the American Counseling Association and the Michigan Counseling Association.

Whether writing or speaking, Sherene is best described as authentic, practical and down-to-earth as she anchors key points with humor and stories and equips individuals to immediately implement ideas and strategies.

An avid believer in living a life she loves, Sherene prizes key relationships. She also loves traveling and being outdoors. In the winter months you'll most likely find her downhill skiing. In the summer she enjoys being out on the water, preferably on something moving really fast.

Sherene can be reached at:

Fully Engaged, LLC

813 North Main #1272

Mt. Pleasant, MI 48804

Phone: 989-621-3763

E-mail: sherene@fullyengaged.us

Website: fullyengaged.us

Book Sherene

Passionate about helping others develop healthier relationships, live life to the fullest and be more effective, Sherene wows audiences with her authentic, high-impact, humorous message based on awareness, acknowledgment, accountability and action.

Participants walk away with practical, hands-on tools that enable them to harness their power, craft a clearer purpose for their lives, experience increased inner peace and reawaken their passions.

As an international speaker, Sherene is uniquely qualified to address audiences of 5 to 5000 and more. She can deliver an inspirational can-do keynote, a content-rich general session, a hands-on workshop, or a retreat.

Depending on your needs, Sherene will personalize a presentation on issues including setting boundaries, creating respectful relationships, resolving conflict, bringing out the best in others, achieving dreams and living life to the fullest.

Her comprehensive, one-of-a kind, life and relationship development philosophy has the right blend of wisdom, strategies and practical ideas that participants can implement immediately.

To discuss how Sherene can best serve your organization, contact:

Fully Engaged, LLC
Phone: 989-621-3763
E-mail: info@fullyengaged.us
Website: fullyengaged.us

Ready to Create a Life You Love...

If you're like most people, achieving your hopes and dreams and creating a life you love doesn't end with a single book or presentation. Set yourself up to stay focused and reach your dreams far more quickly by working with a success coach.

Success Coaching will help you:

♦ Clarify what's most important to you.
♦ Organize your life around your top values.
♦ Navigate relationships.
♦ Refocus when you get off track.
♦ Reduce stress, tension and fatigue.
♦ Overcome distractions and things that hold you back.
♦ De-clutter your life.
♦ Stay energized, encouraged and engaged.
♦ Turn your dreams into reality.

If you'd like to:

♦ Work with a *Pick* Success Coach.
♦ Attend a *Pick* seminar or retreat.
♦ Host a *Pick* seminar or retreat.
♦ Lead or join a *Pick* Group.
♦ Become a *Pick* Success Coach.

To pick up the pace on realizing your dreams, contact:
Fully Engaged, LLC
Phone: 989-621-3763
E-mail: pickupthepace@fullyengaged.us